People, Peregrines and Arctic Pipelines

The critical battle to build Canada's northern gas pipelines.

Donald Peacock

J. J. Douglas Ltd.

VANCOUVER

J. J. Douglas Ltd.
1875 Welch Street
North Vancouver, Canada
V7P 1B7

Canadian Cataloguing in Publication Data

Peacock, Donald.
  People, peregrines and Arctic pipelines

ISBN 0-88894-138-2

1. Gas, Natural — Pipe lines — Environmental
aspects — Arctic regions. 2. Wildlife
conservation — Arctic regions. I. Title.
TD195.P5P42   333.8'2   C77-002071-2

Designed by Mike Yazzolino
Typesetting by Compeer Typographic Services, Toronto

Printed and bound in Canada by The Hunter Rose Company

To Drew, and again to Frances, Tony and Danielle

CONTENTS

PREFACE

The story of Arctic gas and the plans to market it in southern Canada and the United States is a long and very complicated one. Most Canadians know more about the controversies reported in the news media over land claims by native people in the Northwest Territories and the Yukon and environmental fears than they do about the actual pipeline proposals.

The issue of native land claims is an important one, as is the impact of pipelines on the Arctic environment. But, assuming that any project is approved by the Canadian government, there is, in my judgment, an even more fundamental issue to be settled: individual freedom and equality of opportunity, though on a far grander scale than usually witnessed. In particular this story is about equality of access to opportunity in business — the very big business of energy, in which power has notoriously been used to reduce freedom and monopolize opportunity. To dismiss this element of the long pipeline drama as economic nationalism is too simplistic and imprecise. Canada's national economic interests are certainly involved, but even more at stake is the right of relative newcomers to an industry — especially in their own country — to an equal chance to compete for project ownership and management control against interests long entrenched and habituated to giving orders, from outside the country.

The Arctic gas pipeline decision by the governments of Canada and the United States brings to a multibillion-dollar climax one of the most dramatic and costly power struggles in the annals of international big business.

It introduces a new test of Canada's economic independence. Will American politics and big business deny Canadians the right of ownership and management control of the pipeline in their own country? Given the chance, will Canadians have the capability to finance, build and operate the Canadian sections of this largest of all privately-constructed pipelines — or will they, finally, have to fall back on American help?

The decision may influence the global balance of power of multinational petroleum corporations, for if Exxon, Gulf and Shell control the Arctic pipeline, some of the power they lost to the Organization of Petroleum Exporting Countries (OPEC) in Arabia and elsewhere, may be recovered in the Arctic. If Canadians own and operate the main sections of the line through Canada, the multinationals are likely to regain less of their lost power.

But the pipeline project is more than another great construction scheme to tame the vast geography of Canada. It symbolizes a new approach to resource development demanded of capitalist enterprise by a general public weary of exploitation for money profits alone. Planners of the pipeline had to take into account the demands of people to know, as well, what the impact might be on the socio-economic situation and the environment. This explains why the two groups which were competing for the right to move Arctic gas south across Canada had spent, by 1977, close to $170 million on pre-construction impact studies and testimony to various public agencies on subjects ranging from native peoples' interests and permafrost problems to protection of the nesting grounds of peregrine falcons, and breeding grounds of caribou and white beluga whales.

One proposal was for a project which, within Canada as well as outside, would be clearly dominated by control from multinational oil companies. The other proposal would give Canadian businessmen undisputed ownership and control of the sections of the project within Canada.

The issue of project selection for Canadians was thus as clearcut as the issue of native land claims. It determined if we would run our own affairs with Canadians making their own decisions independently, or if we were to take orders from foreigners, primarily for the benefit of another country.

This book was written and published with financial assistance from the Alberta Gas Trunk Line Company Limited of Calgary, a major participant in one of the competing proposals for moving natural gas south by pipeline from the Arctic regions of Alaska and northwestern Canada. But the aid was accepted by me and by the publisher only with the clear understanding that the book would be written from my independent research and could be published even if my conclusions did not support the Alberta Gas Trunk Line Company's position. This freedom, enhanced by the unconditional financial help, has been fully employed in the production of the book. If the result does not please everyone, the responsibility is entirely mine.

I undertook to write the book against a very demanding deadline (roughly three months were available for research and writing) because I believe that the issues raised by the Arctic pipeline proposals are of great importance to all Canadians, and yet they are not as clearly understood as they ought to be. Hopefully, this book will contribute something towards improving this understanding.

1

THE COSTLIEST PIPELINE

The idea for a pipeline to carry natural gas from Alaska and the Mackenzie River Delta to markets in southern Canada and the U.S. was initiated in 1970. It grew from a study begun in 1967 for a pipeline from the southwestern Northwest Territories. The pipeline rivalled in cost, complexity and controversy the building of the Canadian Pacific Railway, the TransCanada pipeline, the St. Lawrence Seaway and the James Bay hydro-power complex. Once again, the imaginations of men in big business were fired by the financial and engineering challenges created by a project of this magnitude. Competition for permission to build an Arctic pipeline resulted, in fact, in the most costly pre-project corporate manoeuvring in the history of the oil — and any other — industry.

The proposal to pipe Arctic natural gas to southern markets in Canada and the United States was billed from the first as the largest single pipeline undertaking ever attempted by private industry. The engineering difficulties of constructing a massive 48-inch diameter pipeline through permafrost to withstand harsh Arctic conditions were formidable. The pipeline length from Prudhoe Bay, Alaska, to the southern border of Canada was estimated at from about 2,500 miles to 2,700 miles, depending on which was approved. Initial cost estimates ranged from $1.5 billion to $2.5 billion, but by early 1977 had risen to between $7.2 billion and

1

more than $12 billion, all contingencies considered. (In its day the Canadian Pacific Railway was built, eventually, for about $100 million, and with a great deal of government help. The Trans-Canada gas pipeline between Alberta and Montreal, at 2,200 miles in length the world's longest to date, cost $370 million and needed $120 million in temporary government financing. The St. Lawrence Seaway, a joint Canadian-American government enterprise, cost a total of $1 billion. Only the James Bay project in northern Quebec is more costly, at an anticipated final price of $30 billion by 1985.)

Like the TransCanada pipeline before it, the Arctic pipeline raised the recurring issue of Canada's economic independence as a nation: Canadian ownership and control of our natural resources and their exploitation, as opposed to American and/or multinational ownership and control. The observation which William Kilbourn made in *Pipeline*, his history of the TransCanada pipeline, still held true:

> I assume that by 1953 Canadians wanted, and were willing to pay a price if necessary, to keep control of a new means of transportation for a new source of energy in their own hands. . . . To protect national sovereignty and maintain a better bargaining position it was preferable to have at least one of Canada's two greatest potential sources of energy under Canadian control. The industry of central Canada would be less completely dependent on American supplies of coal and natural gas or upon seaborne petroleum and liquid natural gas brought in by tanker to the port of Montreal.

The TransCanada pipeline also took a long time to plan and finance, and suffered many setbacks before it became a reality. It now carries gas across Canada from Alberta to the industrial markets of Ontario and Quebec, but legislation enabling the company to build the pipeline caused one of the most bitter debates in the history of the Canadian House of Commons before it passed, with the rare use of debate closure, in the spring of 1956. The Liberal government which employed this power was defeated in the election the following year, and its fall was largely blamed on its gross mishandling of the TransCanada PipeLines Limited legislation. So pipeline politics, such as those which swirled around plans to bring Arctic gas south, were nothing new in Canada. Nor were the political dangers to a government mishandling pipeline

2

issues any less now than in 1956. In fact, they were probably greater.

The primary issue was whether, despite the certainty of its economic benefits, the pipeline should be built at all. This was partly because of modern doubt about the value of economic progress for its own sake, and partly a fear about environmental and sociological consequences. But if there was to be an Arctic pipeline, many other questions arose. Should the pipeline be built across Alaska or across Canada? If it was decided that the pipeline should be built across Canada, as seemed most likely, which of the competing routes should it follow? Or should the regulatory agencies recommend to their governments that an altogether different project should be built? And if the pipeline was built through Canada, by whom should it be built — individual Canadian companies which would own and be responsible for various sections of it? An all-Canadian consortium responsible for the entire project within Canada? Or an international consortium, in which decisive power almost certainly would be retained in American-based multinational hands? This latter issue itself broke down into a more localized Canadian issue, too — should an Arctic gas pipeline across Canada be built by a consortium dominated from Calgary or from Toronto?

Supply and Demand
Further complicating the pipeline decision was a complex combination of factors related to the supply and demand of energy: the drastic shift in world petroleum power as a result of actions by OPEC; the confusing effect of changing estimates of the gas reserves on which the idea of an Arctic pipeline had been based; and the energy crisis experienced by the United States during the winter of 1976-77, which made the need for a pipeline from Alaska urgent.

When serious thought was first being given to the possibility of piping Arctic gas south, the gas then being discovered in Canada's Mackenzie Delta region was thought to be surplus to Canadian needs. It was therefore considered available for export to the U.S., along with gas from the North Slope of Alaska overlooking Prudhoe Bay in the Arctic Ocean. It was also assumed at that time that the larger Arctic gas production would come first from the Canadian wells and later from the wells in Alaska. So it seemed then, to almost everyone involved, to make eminent sense to build one large single pipeline capable of carrying the gas from both regions to markets in the lower 48 American states.

However, this was back in the days when world oil supplies seemed inexhaustible and prices were influenced, if not directly controlled, by the seven largest multinational oil companies (nicknamed "The Seven Sisters"): Exxon (Esso), Gulf, Texaco, Mobil and Socal (Chevron) from the United States; Shell and British Petroleum (BP) from Europe. At that time, the major problem of the Canadian petroleum industry was finding markets; oil from many of the countries which now are members of OPEC was available as cheaply in Canada's petroleum heartland of Alberta as oil from the province's own wells. During the early 1960s, light Arabian crude oil sold at the source (FOB) for an average price of $1.25 per barrel. Throughout the 1960s petroleum energy prices declined in relation to the prices of other goods and services, until by 1970 the price of light Arabian crude had dropped to about $1.20 per barrel.

Canadian consumers, individual, commercial and institutional, were major beneficiaries of this exploitation of Arabian resources for more than a decade. Between 1961 and 1970, for instance, the average cost of energy to individual consumers in Canada decreased by about 20 per cent relative to the most widely used yardstick of living costs, the Consumer Price Index. For commercial and institutional users, energy costs declined by about 10 per cent on the same relative basis during the same period. The cost of energy to Canadian manufacturing companies declined by 8 per cent during this period, relative to the Consumer Price Index, and by 30 per cent relative to wage rates. (*An Energy Strategy for Canada*, Ottawa, 1976, p.8)

Then came a dramatic example of the interconnection of events that so often makes today's world, economically at least, a single community. The aftermath of a war in the distant Middle East during October 1973 transformed the energy situation of Canada and every nation, industrial or otherwise. Indeed, the entire world economy was changed beyond recognition when the member-states of OPEC succeeded in driving the world price of crude oil up to about $11 per barrel — roughly nine times the price of a barrel of light Arabian crude in 1970. (By May 1977 the price had reached $14.50 per barrel.)

Suddenly, industrial nations such as Canada and the United States were vigorously reviewing energy resources.

4

During 1974 and 1975, as the world adjusted to the shock of the OPEC takeover of oil pricing from the multinational oil companies, Canada's National Energy Board made an exhaustive review of Canadian reserves. The conclusion which the board drew from its review of gas supply and anticipated future demand was that Canada did not have as much to spare as previously thought. The Mackenzie Delta's gas, which had been considered surplus to Canada's needs and therefore available for export to the more needy United States market, was then looked upon as essential to meet Canadian needs — and soon. In an astonishing reversal of earlier expectations, the NEB anticipated that production from southern Canadian sources of natural gas, mainly in Alberta, would begin to fall short of Canadian requirements by the late 1970s.

Planners of gas pipelines south from the Arctic began to proceed on this new assumption, but by 1976 both this and another basic assumption had to be revised again. The amount of gas available from sources in southern Canada, primarily Alberta, was becoming larger than anticipated, while the discoveries of new gas supplies in the Mackenzie Delta were falling short of earlier expectations. Further complicating the pipeliners' plans was an unexpected decline in demand for natural gas, caused in part by the powerful upward push on prices by OPEC, by a rising chorus of exhortations for energy conservation beginning about the same time, by a slowing down of the economy in 1974 and 1975, and by warmer-than-usual winter weather from 1973 through 1975.

Then, in the winter of 1976-77, the United States experienced the worst weather in decades. The increase in the use of gas to heat homes caused gas shortages which forced the closure of factories, businesses and schools, with consequent layoffs of more than two million workers in some 20 states. The impact of the shortage led magazines such as *Newsweek* to report that the U.S. had been brought to "a natural-gas crisis every bit as serious as the 1973 Arab oil embargo." The 1977 crisis underlined the fact that natural gas was the most important single source of energy in use in the United States. About half of America's homes and 40 per cent of its industries depended for their energy on natural gas, which accounted for 30 per cent of U.S. energy consumption. In Canada, gas provided about 20 per cent of all energy consumed.

Ironically, while the U.S. was learning how urgently it needed a connection with the Alaska gas, Canada was learning that its need for Arctic gas was less urgent than previously thought. The review of gas reserves in southern Canada showed that they could meet Canadian requirements comfortably until perhaps 1985 or later. Previously, they had been expected to run short at least five years earlier.

Environmental, Ecological and People Issues
Other issues were also very important, especially in Canada. These included ecological and environmental issues, and — perhaps as important as any other — the issue of aboriginal land rights in the Mackenzie River valley and Delta region, through which both projects proposed to build. These issues received a major proportion of the attention of the National Energy Board during the 18 months of its hearings on the project, to the end of May 1977. The same was true of the Federal Power Commission's 20 months of sittings on the project which ended in April 1977. Consideration of these issues was the sole purpose of the 20 months of hearings held by the Mackenzie Valley Pipeline Inquiry under Mr. Justice Thomas Berger, which wound up in November 1976. A committee of the Canadian House of Commons also investigated the pipeline issues, as did a committee of the U.S. Congress. The pipeline applicants themselves spent millions of dollars on studies unprecedented in the annals of business, intending to anticipate every conceivable problem in these three areas with acceptable solutions.

Yet, for all this effort, no easy consensus emerged on which government could, with political safety, base a final decision about the Arctic pipeline project. As Mr. Justice Berger observed at the end of his hearings in the Katimavik Room of Yellowknife's Explorer Hotel: when they began in March 1975, the opinion of Northerners about the pipeline was split, and it remained divided at the end. The same could truly be said of opinion about the pipeline in the rest of Canada, in Alaska, and in the rest of the United States.

No one involved in this project any longer questioned the fact that there must be a net positive benefit from the pipeline for Northerners, both native peoples and others. Long before his report was issued, Mr. Justice Berger several times evinced a special sympathy for native interests in this project, which could be tantamount to taking an industrial revolution to some northern areas for the first time. Some natives would welcome the pipeline and its accompanying economic benefits, but others feared, he said, "a tearing of the social fabric, the devastation of the land and the loss of their collective identity as a people." He stated that this did not necessarily mean that the pipeline should not be built, but that the native peoples were determined that if it was built, they should benefit from land claims, jobs and in other ways.

In a February 1977 speech to the Canadian Mining Association in Ottawa, Berger said that the Canadian government faces hard choices before deciding whether the Mackenzie Valley pipeline should be built. If the government did decide that the pipeline was in the national interest, said Berger, "we owe it to the peoples of the North and to future generations to take a hard-nosed look at the consequences before we go ahead." He added: "My job is to see that we do."

Power Struggles

During our brief and infrequent interviews, Robert Blair showed a characteristic reluctance to appear as a hero. But the record clearly shows that it was his decision, taken in Calgary early in 1970, to thrust his company into the Arctic gas pipeline action which spurred into being the titanic intercorporate power struggle between Canadian and multinational companies that the project bids for approval finally became. Any competition for the right to build *any* pipeline *anywhere*, much less the potentially longest and most costly of them all, was previously unheard of, if not unimaginable. (Early in the campaign for the TransCanada pipeline, for example, the then Canadian Minister of Trade, C. D. Howe, summoned the two interested groups to his Ottawa office and told them to merge or else. They promptly merged.) The normal course is that one application is made to the appropriate government agency, the agency examines the application and then, with or without requiring revisions, approves it, whereupon the pipeline is built.

Blair's decision turned a pipeline planning study into one of the fiercest competitions in oil industry annals. From the beginning, his insistence upon Canadian dominance of Canadian sections of any pipeline made him an outsider to the international consortium he first tried unsuccessfully to join, later won acceptance to, then withdrew from in disappointment, and finally openly fought to the finish. As a result, Blair's activities have been more varied than those of his competitors and require more attention to describe and explain. While his opponents established their position in 1970 and largely remained with it, Blair kept circling their encampment and attempting sallies in search of a winning opening for his own forces. Being more extensive than those of his opponents, Blair's activities in this drama have in places required more space to cover.

In the end there were three groups of applicants competing to move the Arctic gas, each in a different way. One, the Canadian-dominated Alaska Highway-Maple Leaf Projects, was headed by Robert Blair, president and chief executive officer of Alberta Gas Trunk Line Company Limited of Calgary. The other, the American-dominated Alaskan-Canadian Arctic Gas Project, was headed by Vernon Horte, president and chief operating officer of Canadian Arctic Gas Pipelines Limited of Toronto. A third application was to liquefy Alaska gas and carry it by ship to the U.S., bypassing Canada. The first two projects were generally thought to be the primary competitors.

The evolution of these two applications towards a final confrontation over stakes worth billions of dollars involved at various stages and in various combinations, many companies, some with worldwide interests. Horte, as then president of TransCanada PipeLines Limited of Toronto, was a key figure from the start. The first feasibility study was carried out in 1967 by a consortium of TransCanada, Michigan Wisconsin Pipe Line Company, and Natural Gas Pipeline Company of America. This group became the Northwest Project Study Group in 1970, when three other American-based multinational companies joined.

Blair had just been appointed vice-president of Alberta Gas Trunk Line when, according to him, he asked in early 1970 whether Alberta Gas could join the Northwest Group and was turned down. Horte did not deny this, but maintained that he no longer remembered such an application, although he conceded that it would have been a likely move on Blair's part. No written evidence was available to support either contention. However, it was a vital move in the pipeline stakes. Blair then formed the Trunk North Project Group to apply to build an Arctic pipeline in competition with Horte's group. Blair strongly believed that any Arctic pipeline crossing Canada should be majority-owned and controlled by Canadians, and that any main Arctic pipeline should be a common carrier, i.e., controlled by a party which was neither a gas producer nor a gas utility purchaser.

The dramatic action, often behind closed corporate doors, but

8

now revealed through some 100,000 pages of hearing transcripts, steadily grew livelier, more complex, and much more confusing, from then on.

Many men in the petroleum industry were more powerful than Robert Blair or Vernon Horte. But they were at the centre of this action when it started, and remained there as it ended. Not by choice but by circumstance, they were gradually thrust into the roles of chief Canadian protagonists — knights of the boardroom, ankle-deep in executive pile, exchanging verbal thunderbolts as the final curtain descended.

Vernon L. Horte is a native of Kingman, Alberta, where he was born 12 July 1925. He graduated from the University of Alberta in 1949 with a B.Sc. in chemical engineering and started his career with Chemical and Geological Laboratories in Edmonton, then joined the Alberta Energy Resources Conservation Board as a gas engineer. In 1952 he moved to the United States to take a position with DeGolyer and McNaughton, a firm of petroleum consulting engineers in Dallas, Texas. Five years later he returned to Canada to work in Calgary for TransCanada PipeLines Limited as chief gas supply engineer, just in time to get in at the very beginning of the northern pipeline play. During nine years with the company in Calgary and one in Toronto, Horte worked his way up to vice-president, and became president in 1968.

S. Robert Blair joined Alberta Gas Trunk Line Company Limited in December 1969 as executive vice-president. In September 1970 he became president and chief executive officer. By then he had been in pipelines for 19 years. Born 13 August 1929 in Trinidad, where his Canadian father was working as a refinery engineer, Bob Blair graduated in 1951 from Queen's University, Kingston, Ontario, with a B.Sc. in chemical engineering. The same year he went to work on construction of the 700-mile 24-inch Trans Mountain oil pipeline across British Columbia from Edmonton, Alberta. In 1959 he joined Alberta and Southern Gas Company Limited of Calgary, a subsidiary of Pacific Gas and Electric Company of San Francisco, and became president seven years later. But even in that position, he found himself taking orders from the American parent. "It was not a good experience," a colleague of Blair's told me. "He didn't like being dictated to from San Francisco."

Both men are of average height and, although he is four years older, there is less gray in Horte's dark hair than in Blair's. But

Blair has more of it, or seems to, because he wears his hair combed forward and long, whereas Horte's is done in the short back and sides style more familiar in the oil patch. Both men have brown eyes which almost always seem to be shining with intense ambition and energy, and sometimes with indignation when they talk about each other.

Both are tough-minded, highly competent and decisive but, in personal conversation, Horte's manner is as offhand and nearly as disarming as Blair's. Horte is conservative and careful, a determined plodder with an engineer's direct, literal approach to problems, a man comfortable with the established structures of business, more ready to defend than to change them. Blair is impulsive and intuitive, practical yet imaginative, a questing challenger of business ways and establishment, ready to take risks on his own judgment, and one to whom personal independence is more important than security. While there is an air of substantial competence about Horte, more creative vibes emanate from Blair, a quality which makes many of his business acquaintances nervous around him: Horte is predictable in their world, Blair is not.

Whatever may be said of Blair's motives, his decision to defy three of the world's largest petroleum multinationals — Exxon, Shell and Gulf — and to try to win these pipeline stakes on his own terms made a fascinating contest out of the process of applying for government permission to build an Arctic gas pipeline. The full extent of this struggle was not widely appreciated, despite the immensity of the issues involved and the power and money of the project backers. For instance, early in the game, the chairman of the National Energy Board, the gentle-natured, judicious-minded but quick-tempered Marshall Crowe, was forced to resign the Board's Arctic pipeline panel. This resulted from a move thought to have been initiated by some multinational corporations which feared that his interest in independent Canadian business enterprise would prove detrimental to their cause.

However, it is clear from records previously unavailable for publication that the catalyst — as troublesome as tireless; some believe for better, others for worse — in this struggle was Alberta Gas Trunk Line, headquartered in Calgary and headed by Bob Blair.

Horte had even more than the immense power and prestige of the world's richest consortium on his side. His group had its own claims of Canadian participation and promised economic and other benefits to Canada.

If Trunk Line had any advantage at all, it might perhaps have been its clear grasp of the new capitalist development ethic which seemed to be unfolding in the planning and building of northern pipelines. It saw the necessity for, and quickly undertook, socio-economic studies of the pipeline's impact on Northerners and their communities, as well as the by now expected studies on the ecosystem and the environment. By the end of 1970, Trunk Line had spent a million dollars of its own money on feasibility studies for the Trunk North Project and committed another three million for 1971. Added to the $12 million already committed by the Northwest Group — not to mention what a third group which moved into the Arctic action from British Columbia planned to spend — this meant that a minimum of $16 million would be invested in learning things about the Arctic that nobody had ever studied before, certainly not in such depth. Some observers were — and still are — sceptical about the purposes of these expenditures, but such a gambling of capital — and this a minimum — was unprecedented both in purpose and size. But this minimum turned out to be miniscule compared to the amounts of money ultimately spent on Arctic gas pipeline feasibility studies: $150 million by Arctic Gas and $42 million by the Foothills group.

Blair and Horte did not agree on the extent to which either's pipeline application fulfilled the new development ethic. Fortunately there are many facts on the record which help in making comparisons, for the implementation of this ethic was an integral element in the two competing applications.

In his famous book *Small is Beautiful*, Ernst F. Schumacher advocated an enterprise ethic devoted more than in the past to development with permanence in mind, instead of temporary exploitation with only material profit as its objective. None of the pipeliners which scrambled to present the most acceptable solutions in the great Arctic gas development drama were in it merely for their selfless love of humanity. But the new power of the politics of ecology, which now does seem to include the human being as the foremost of the organisms to be considered, was destined to be a major factor in choosing the winning applicant.

There was far more at stake, of course, than the fortunes of the three competing groups that wanted to build the pipeline. In the first place, the vital interests of two countries, Canada and the United States, were directly involved in the pipeline decision. Thus the final decision had to be worked out jointly between the Canadian and American governments and their agencies, the National Energy Board in Ottawa and the Federal Power Commission in Washington. The need to connect the United States with new sources of gas supply was certain to be a dominant factor in the decisions, especially in Washington.

After the severe winter of 1976 with the resulting gas shortage in the U.S., there was a strong feeling in Ottawa and in Washington that a decision had to be made soon to allow a pipeline to be built across Canada to carry Alaskan gas to the lower 48 states, whatever might be decided about the transport of gas from the Canadian Arctic. The strength of this feeling was reflected in remarks by Prime Minister Pierre Trudeau in the House of Commons on 24 February 1977, following his visit to President Jimmy Carter in Washington. Trudeau said that the Canadian government would try to make a decision about an Arctic gas pipeline by September 1977, out of a desire to co-operate with President Carter. The President was required by a law which Congress passed in 1976 to make a decision by 1 September 1977 on competing proposals to ship Alaskan gas to the lower 48 states. Trudeau said that no assurances were given Carter as to which of the competing proposals Canada might approve, but he hoped that some decision would be made by September 1977 to help Americans get Arctic gas as soon as possible.

A treaty clearing the way for these decisions was signed between Canada and the United States in Washington on 28 January 1977. In the treaty, each nation undertook not to interfere with the transit across its territory of the other's natural gas and oil.

2

CONTENDERS EMERGE

The petroleum industry learned some expensive lessons during the battle for approval of the Alyeska pipeline. These lessons played an important part in the evolution of the two competing proposals for an Arctic gas pipeline.

Exploitation of energy resources has rarely, if ever, been dominated by a concern for society or even for nationalism, much less the modern concern for ecological balance and environmental quality. However, a new capitalist development ethic is emerging from the conflict raging between conservationists and developers of natural resources. It is not an ethic that represents radical change, or anything like the last improvement that capitalism needs. Nor is it an ethic that the petroleum industry has accepted willingly; it has been imposed by the power of democratically aroused public opinion. It is an ethic whose evolution has been far too slow and whose still uncertain emergence is long overdue. All that this new capitalist ethic entails is the inclusion in resource development of a previously neglected concern for legitimate human interests in what the impact may be on the socio-economic situation and the environment.

The conservationists only recently began to be supported by public and political demands that a more ethical approach than in the past be given practical application to new resource development. This public opposition appeared in full force for the first time soon after plans were announced in February 1969 for the

Alyeska line, an oil pipeline across Alaska. Probably no single energy development project had ever been subjected to so much opposition — and often successful opposition — by environmentalists as the Alyeska pipeline was.

The Alyeska Pipeline
In 1968 the Atlantic Richfield Company of Los Angeles discovered oil and natural gas at Prudhoe Bay, Alaska. It brought in a well on the North Slope of Alaska that tested at the healthy but not unusually high output of more than 3,500 barrels of oil and 4 million cubic feet of natural gas per day. A second well drilled seven miles southeast of the initial one was also successful, and the Arctic petroleum boom was on. In September of the next year, the State of Alaska offered for bids leases on some 450,000 acres of North Slope land and permafrost. Despite the desolate isolation of the area, the winning bids added up to some $900 million (U.S.). This was 50 per cent more than the previous record single sale of petroleum leases anywhere else in the world. Among the most successful bidders were representatives of four of the world's largest petroleum companies: Exxon, Shell, British Petroleum, and Gulf. All four are members of the group of multinational companies, nicknamed ''The Seven Sisters,'' that has long dominated the world petroleum scene.

The establishment of the Alyeska Pipeline Service Company by BP, Atlantic Richfield and Humble, all major holders of Alaska oil and gas reserves, gave them a significant role in Arctic pipelines. The plan was to build 789.1 miles of 48-inch pipeline across Alaska from Prudhoe Bay in the north to the ice-free Pacific port of Valdez on the south coast. The cost estimate started at $1.5 billion and soon rose to $2.5 billion. Until the Arctic gas pipeline plans appeared, the Alyeska line was billed by the *Anchorage Daily Times* as ''the largest construction job ever undertaken by private industry in the free world.'' An Associated Press news agency story said that the line had been ''envisioned by its planners as history's greatest engineering feat.'' (By completion in 1977, the Alyeska line was expected to cost $7.7 billion, roughly five times its initial estimate. This works out to $9.6 million per mile, compared to Arctic Gas cost estimates in terms of 1976 prices of between $3 million and $4 million per mile; about 40 per cent of Alyeska's actual costs through similar terrain.) As the figures show, although the Alyeska construction was on schedule pretty

14

well, the actual costs far overran the estimates. At the peak of construction, the Alyeska line was expected to employ 16,000 men; actually, this reached something over 22,000 (compared to 5,000 at the peak of CPR construction).

The enormousness of this anticipated achievement seemed to impress almost no one except its proponents. Most Alaskans seemed far more excited about the prospects of new income for their state, from royalties and other economic spinoffs, once the oil began to flow. The pipeline company quickly became involved in costly litigation involving environmental issues, Alaska state government royalty demands, and native peoples' land claims.

The environmentalists opposed the pipeline on two main grounds: the danger of pollution from pipeline breaks, and the risk of oil spills by the supertankers which were destined to carry the oil from Valdez south along the Canadian coastline to refineries in Washington State.

The Arctic ecosystem is both the most desolate and the most delicate on earth, because of the long months during which it lies in the limbo of brutal cold. This period of long immobility means that the ecosystem recovers slowly from damage. Moss displaced as surface cover, for instance, takes 50 years to grow back and become insulation for permafrost (permanently frozen mixture of ice and soil) from the melting summer sun. The risks in the pipeline plan were, beyond much doubt, greater than for any pipeline built before. It would be carrying hot oil at about 170 degrees F. across terrain that not only comprised long sections of permafrost, but also was prone to earthquakes. Such risks drew intense attention from environmentalists and attracted wide public interest.

These considerations were behind the application for an injunction against the pipeline's construction. The application was filed under a new U.S. National Environmental Policy Act by five groups working together: the Friends of the Earth, the Wilderness Society, the Environmental Defence Fund, the Cordova District Fisheries Union, and the Canadian Wildlife Federation. Judge George Hart, Jr., of the U.S. Federal District Court in Washington granted the injunction in April 1970, just as the two Arctic gas pipeline proposals were being developed.

In April 1969, the confident new Alyeska Pipeline Service Company had ordered $100 million worth of Japanese-made 48-inch steel pipe. By the time that injunction was granted, many

ALYESKA   PROJECT

TERRITORIES

TRANSCANADA PIPELINES

Winnipeg

Emerson

Quebec City

Montreal

Ottawa

GREAT LAKES

MIDWESTERN

Toronto

tons of the pipe had been flown in workhorse Hercules aircraft to the North Slope and stacked in huge piles, ready for an early go-ahead on the pipeline construction. Now, all activity slowly ground to a halt across the North Slope. The Alaska state government's eager expectation of a new era of prosperity was dashed. Would the $900 million that the oil companies had paid in September 1969 for North Slope leases keep the state solvent until these astonishing new obstacles to resource development were overcome, and the oil — and the money — finally flowed?

Alyeska Pipeline officials found themselves testifying before committees of the U.S. House of Representatives and Senate about issues that had never troubled pipeliners before. Their project reports included an earthquake study. They carried out tests on reseeding disturbed Arctic ground cover. Test facilities simulating hot pipeline through the permafrost were established on the North Slope and in Fairbanks. A study was made of the socio-economic impact their project would have on Alaska. A grid map was prepared depicting every inch of the construction project. An oil spill contingency plan was commissioned for the port of Valdez.

In 1971, Congress had granted Alaska's 60,000 native peoples (Eskimos, Indians and Aleuts) historic land claims which gave them the right to a share in development income from 40 million acres in the state. The Native Land Claims Act also granted the native peoples $1 billion in cash annuity. The interested oil companies, eager to get the land question out of the way, were said to have spent millions lobbying in support of the settlement.

The U.S. Department of the Interior, meanwhile, was feverishly developing a rebuttal to the environmentalists' arguments against the pipeline. By March 1972, the department had spent $10 million on its research: the evidence supporting the pipeline, and a list of construction and operation stipulations (the Environmental Impact Statement) which filled nine volumes. Judge Hart took until August 1972 to digest this statement, and ruled that the Arctic environment which the Alyeska Pipeline Company proposed to cross seemed assured of adequate protection. He lifted the injunction.

The environmentalists refused to surrender. Their numbers now included — along with such individuals as David Anderson, then leader of the Liberal party of British Columbia — the Sierra Club, with past-president Dr. Edgar Wayburn co-ordinating its Alaska program. They continued to state their environmental predictions, but they also took up a new line of argument. A technicality in the 1920 Mineral Leasing Act stipulated that a pipeline right-of-way across public land should not exceed 25 feet on either side of the pipeline itself. In the case of Alyeska's 48-inch pipeline, this would provide a total allowable width of 54 feet. However, Interior Secretary Rogers C. B. Morton had complied with Alyeska's request for extra room to accommodate the massive equipment that would be needed to build its line by issuing a special permit allowing Alyeska a right-of-way as wide as 150 feet during construction.

Since all parties agreed that the Alyeska line could not be built on the width of land stipulated by existing law, the U.S. Circuit Court of Appeals ruled in February 1973 that there was no choice but to enjoin issuance of Morton's special permit. Congress would either have to amend the law to allow a greater width or exempt this project from the law's provisions. To the disappointment of the environmentalists, the court declined to rule on their environmental issues, since the ruling on the technicality made these issues moot. They had hoped for a favourable ruling on these issues, too.

Dr. Wayburn hailed the decision as a "clear rebuff to the oil companies" and was quoted by the *Anchorage Daily Times* as saying that it provided "a fresh opportunity to plan wisely . . . allowing for a proper development while protecting the fragile environment." In Victoria, British Columbia, an elated David Anderson said that the Alyeska line was "stopped dead as of now." Both men proved to have been premature in their optimism.

In November 1973, Congress amended the right-of-way legislation and removed all other remaining obstacles to the pipeline. Its construction was set to start by 1 July 1974. Under a system of royalties negotiated by Alaska Governor William Egan's administration, the state government expected to receive about $300 million a year from North Slope production when the pipeline was completed in 1977. The cost, in 1973, had been estimated to run as high as $4.5 billion, and each year of delay was said to have increased the cost by $200 million to $400 million.

Reaction to the go-ahead of the Alyeska line of Alaska remained mixed, though by far the majority seemed to support it. Bumper stickers could be seen everywhere that automobiles could drive in the state, bearing the words: "Sierra Club, Go Home." But Emil Notti, who ran unsuccessfully for Congress as a Democrat in 1972 and helped to lead his fellow Alaskan native people's fight for the land claims settlement, commented: "I'm not convinced that development is going to be automatically good for Alaska. . . . It's not planned. It's just happening." (*Calgary Herald* 8 November 1973; reprint from *Washington Post*)

The decision, like every political decision, was bound to evoke disappointment. Weighing the pros and cons, which included worrisome forecasts of early energy shortages in the U.S. if new supply sources were not soon established, Congress chose the immediate wrath of the environmentalists over the future wrath of a nation short of energy.

In view of the costly and disruptive gas shortages that developed in the U.S. in 1976, the decision does not seem all that unwise. And at the time it was made, there was, after all, the Interior Department's nine volumes of evidence that enough wise planning had already been done to allow for a proper pipeline development in Alaska, while protecting its fragile Arctic environment.

The Northwest Project: The First Contender

At about the same time as the Prudhoe Bay field was discovered, the three pipeline companies — one Canadian and two American — backing the study begun in September 1967 realized that the hope of finding large new quantities of gas in the southwestern region of the Northwest Territories was not going to be fulfilled, certainly in the near future. New discoveries were too small to make a pipeline to southern markets from there feasible. But in 1969, the same year in which the Alyeska Pipeline Service Company had announced its controversial project, Panarctic Oils Limited of Calgary, owned in minority part (45 per cent) by the Canadian government and in majority part by private corporations, discovered considerable gas and some oil in Canada's Arctic islands.

Early in 1969 the three pipeline companies — Michigan Wisconsin Pipe Line Company, Detroit; Natural Gas Pipeline Company of America, Chicago; and TransCanada PipeLines Limited, Toronto — therefore decided to expand the study to include a possible pipeline extending to the Mackenzie River Delta of northwestern Canada and the North Slope of Alaska. They also took on three more partners, all of them American companies: the Atlantic Richfield Company, the Standard Oil Company (Sohio) of Cleveland, and Humble Oil & Refining Company of New York City, a subsidiary of Exxon. True to what by now was an old

20

petroleum industry tradition, the world's largest multinationals had already begun to move in to try to take control from wellhead to consumer.

The six companies called their new consortium the Northwest Project Study Group. In a July 1970 statement, the three newcomers were described as "producers of oil and gas having major interests in the reserves being developed on the North Slope of Alaska." They were seeking an outlet for their products, and the three pipeline companies wanted additional gas supplies for their customers. (Since then, Canadian subsidiaries of Exxon, Gulf and Shell have become major holders of gas reserves in Canada's Mackenzie Delta, too.)

The enormousness of the present Arctic pipeline project was already evident in the very first estimates put forth by the Northwest Project Study Group in the July 1970 statement. The pipeline was to be about 2,500 miles long, use pipe up to 48 inches in diameter (larger than used in any previous North American gas pipeline), carry 3 billion cubic feet of gas per day when fully powered with 1.5 million compressor horsepower, and cost about $2.5 billion (U.S.) to build. The statement pointed out that at a cost of $2.5 billion, the pipeline under study "would be the largest construction project ever undertaken by private industry." (This was before the James Bay project.) This did not include the cost of related facilities that would be required to move the gas to markets in eastern Canada, particularly Ontario, and across the border into the United States. These, said the statement, "will undoubtedly require several hundreds of millions of dollars in addition." There was also a note of what today seems to have been naive optimism. If studies showed that the pipeline was possible, the Northwest Group anticipated it would be delivering "large volumes" of Arctic gas to the midwestern U.S. and eastern Canada by 1976. The group hastened to emphasize the enormous challenge being undertaken:

It should be emphasized at the outset, however, that the Study Group is not now announcing that the Northwest Project will be built or even that governmental approvals will be sought for that purpose. Neither our group nor anyone else is in a position now to say that a project of this scope and magnitude is feasible or financeable or to announce early construction plans.

All that the group was saying then was that preliminary studies justified more definitive studies, testing and planning. Only when more was learned from those efforts might a specific project be submitted for approval by governmental agencies of Canada and the United States.

From the beginning, the nature of the feasibility studies, even more than the size, set the projected Arctic gas pipeline apart in the experience of the world petroleum industry. The Northwest Project partners were already planning to spend $12 million on feasibility studies. Three of the four categories listed in the statement were familiar to pipeline planners of the past: engineering and design, gas reserves and availability, and financing and economic feasibility. The fourth category was new to pipeline planners, but was already becoming recognized as probably the most important of all from now on: "ecological investigations."

On this last category of studies, the group statement said:

> One of the most important aspects of the Phase II studies — one which will vitally affect the ultimate engineering and design of the Northwest Project — is the study and evaluation of ecological and environmental factors. We recognize that this project cannot be approved or constructed until we have demonstrated to ourselves and the respective governmental agencies involved that the route selection, engineering design and construction procedures would meet necessary requirements for the protection of indigenous wildlife and ecology of the areas it would traverse and that other environmental considerations have been fully taken into account.

No mention was made, however, of socio-economic studies to anticipate the impact of such a project on the inhabitants of the North.

The statement's new emphasis on ecological concerns reflected the growing success of movements demanding greater concern for preserving a humane and habitable environment. This new political pressure in the United States and Canada had begun to make itself felt strongly on governments. No doubt Atlantic Richfield and Humble, which were also involved in the Alyeska Pipeline Company that was still battling ecologists at this time, had been quick to learn from their unusual Alaskan experience.

The eagerness of the Northwest Group to recognize the new power of ecology politics showed in some of the rhetoric which it used. The group's July 1970 statement acknowledged that any construction "will to some extent affect the Arctic environment." The group was also confident, the statement went lyrically on, that its project would be entirely consistent with the "basic conservation objectives" of using natural resources "to the greatest benefit of the greatest number of people."

The changing development ethic reflected in the use of such words is all the more noteworthy when the ancestry of at least one of the group's members is recalled. Humble Oil, a subsidiary of Exxon, was a direct descendant of the Standard Oil Trust of the first John D. Rockefeller. It was this very trust, as British writer Anthony Sampson has noted in his book *The Seven Sisters*, which provoked the anti-trust movement and the machinery of Congressional investigation which has pursued the American oil industry ever since. Given the reputation that the industry has been trying to live down since the first Rockefeller, it is no wonder that there are still a few sceptics to this day about the conversion indicated in the Northwest Group statement.

The Trunk North Project: The Second Contender

Any of the world's major oil companies not already exploring Alberta were attracted to the province by the discovery of oil in large quantities at Leduc in 1947. That and subsequent discoveries made Alberta the source it is today of roughly 80 per cent of all the oil and gas used in Canada, and most of such exports as are still being made to the United States.

When the Alberta government set up the Alberta Gas Trunk Line Company Limited in 1954, it was not welcomed by the oil companies, especially the large multinationals: they were accustomed to owning such facilities themselves, along with the wells producing the products which they carried. The legislation establishing Trunk Line assigned it to operate pipelines as a common carrier of gas within the province. Alberta thus became one of the few places on earth where the producers did not own the gas gathering system, although initially they still maintained control of it. Trunk Line was established as a private company with seven directors, two representing the Alberta government, and a clear majority of five representing the gas producers and utility companies.

Trunk Line was set up purposely to give Canadians, and more particularly Alberta Canadians, some direct influence over development of gas resources in the province. The original offering of 2,552,320 Class "A" common shares at $5.25 each thus was confined to residents of Alberta. The provincial government's treasury branches, banks and brokers were swamped with applications from nearly 100,000 Albertans. Many later sold their shares at a profit. In a brief prepared by Dianne Narvik, Trunk Line vice-president for administration, for the Royal Commission on Corporate Concentration, the company reported that as of October 1975, majority ownership lay within other areas of Canada — though no individual or institution held a controlling block of shares. "However," the brief added, "we believe that in terms of the number of shareholders, the Company has the largest number of Albertan shareholders of any company operating in Canada." This still holds.

Given its background and history, Trunk Line was obviously destined to play an important role in Canada's as well as Alberta's energy economy. Still, whether it finally be treated as wisdom or folly, creative courage or personal ambition carried to excess, Bob Blair's move to thrust Alberta Gas Trunk Line into the Arctic gas pipeline stakes was an uphill battle from the beginning. But written records show that, from the beginning, though their campaign tactics often showed elements of improvisation as the struggle unfolded, the Trunk Line executives were always clear about their main purpose. This remains today as it was spelled out in papers establishing the Trunk North Project in April 1970.

One of Blair's primary beliefs is that all of any Arctic pipeline crossing Canada should be majority owned and controlled by Canadians. This was spelled out in his own preliminary project outline dated 14 April 1970. It said that equity in the new federally chartered company planned for the Yukon-Northwest Territories section of the line should be "issued to Canadian public and Canadian companies, with safeguards to keep control in Canada." The purpose of this control was "to promote and protect Canadian interests in the development of Northern Canadian gas supply areas and of Canadian markets whose demands can appropriately be met by delivery of gas from the new facilities." Canadian-controlled facilities should as well "provide a reliable transport service across Canada for transporting gas produced in Alaska to United States markets." (This objective was repeated in the 19 March 1971 agreement which brought Canadian National Railways into the Trunk North Project study group, and remained to the end a dominant feature of the two-pipeline proposal which

Blair put before the regulatory bodies of Canada and the U.S. in opposition to the single-pipeline proposal of Horte's Arctic Gas group.)

The other objective to which Blair attached primary importance was that any main pipeline from the Arctic south should be a common carrier — not owned and controlled by either the gas producers in the North or their southern customers. The purpose of this objective was spelled out in a revision of the project outline dated 30 April 1970. The wording was careful, but what it meant was that, by keeping a pipeline a common carrier, all producers at one end and all consumers at the other would be kept on an equal competitive basis. Sellers or buyers or a group of both in control of a pipeline serving any area would enjoy an obvious advantage over their competitors in that area who would have no say in the pipeline's operation.

Blair's April 30 Trunk North concept included two other important points. One was that in building an Arctic pipeline south, "the fullest possible use of all facilities which now exist or are contemplated in the near term" should be made. This would minimize or defer capital expenditures. The other was intended to provide opportunities for new economic developments along the pipeline route. "The pipeline service company in each section," Blair wrote, "is to have contractual power to buy any gas from the main line at cost for supply of local consumers and development of local industry along the route."

The Trunk North Project soon had its own feasibility studies under way, covering the same general areas as the Northwest Project Group: engineering design, financing, ecology and environment. The Trunk North studies also included "commitments respecting training of Northern residents," along with the appointment of an independent Environmental Protection Board to ensure a maximum of objectivity in study findings in this interest area. This brought a new challenge into the picture — a "people challenge" of an extent never coped with by pipeliners before.

The common carrier issue had arisen early in negotiations which Blair opened with TransCanada PipeLines. At a 22 April 1970 meeting in their Toronto Commerce Court East offices with Horte and another TransCanada executive, G. W. Woods, Blair invited the Toronto company, as a buyer and shipper of gas, to use the project he proposed for supply from the Northwest Territories and other prospective northern gas sources. Eight days later, Blair, in a written report, said that Horte had expressed appreciation for the forthright disclosure of the Trunk North Project's plans and had expressed interest in further discussions with Blair and other Trunk North executives.

Horte had also asked whether TransCanada would be afforded an equity position in the new company to be set up for transporting gas across the northern territories. Blair wrote:

> My reply discouraged that prospect, on the grounds that while TransCanada is a well-established and Canadian company, it would be better in principle to avoid any equity ownership or representation of any shipper if the transport service company is to maintain the complete autonomy to act as a neutral and common carrier, which we believe to be appropriate.

During those early months, the negotiating crew of Trunk Line was almost constantly on the move. The main members, besides Blair, were Robin J. Abercrombie, vice-president and manager of special studies: Gordon W. Walker, vice-president for operations; and D. H. (Howie) Hushion, vice-president for engineering. They were constantly on the long-distance telephone to potential Arctic gas suppliers, Canadian and American customers, and participants in their project. At the drop of the slightest hint of interest, they would fly across the continent and back for a single interview.

On March 2, Blair and Abercrombie flew to Los Angeles for a secret meeting with utility presidents Jack Horton of Southern California Edison Company and Joseph Rensch of Pacific Lighting Gas Company. Neither company had ever previously shown an interest in buying western Canada gas, but both were then negotiating to buy gas from the southwestern region of the Northwest Territories. Horton and Rensch discussed moving the gas through Alberta Gas Trunk Line facilities — a prospect that petered out with the hopes of finding gas in that region in commercial quantities.

One of the earliest and most consistently helpful sources of interest in the Trunk North Project was a major holder of Alaskan North Slope reserves, British Petroleum — the multinational firm into which Winston Churchill, as First Lord of the Admiralty, bought a 51-per-cent interest for the British government at the start of World War I. This interest the British government has maintained ever since. Blair and Abercrombie flew to New York City for their first meeting with BP Alaska executives on March 31. Those on the BP side included the president, Frank Rickwood, and another executive, Phil Ford. "We found a strong affirmative response in this meeting," Blair wrote in a report a week later. There had been "a particular sense of urgency in BP toward developing a project which could be ready concurrently with the start of North Slope oil production." The meeting with BP Alaska encouraged the Trunk North planners to write immediately to other producers in the area with a similar approach.

Early in May 1970, Blair attended a meeting in the office of the Premier at the Alberta Legislative Assembly building, an austere, domed, stone edifice overlooking the North Saskatchewan River in Edmonton. Others who were present besides then Premier Harry E. Strom were Mines and Minerals Minister A. R. Patrick; Attorney-General Edgar Gerhart; Patrick's deputy, H. H. Somerville; and the chairman of the province's Oil and Gas Conservation Board, G. W. Govier. The purpose was to hear more about the Trunk North study project that Blair had so energetically set in motion the previous month. Now he had to convince the people in his own province, in the very Alberta government that had established Trunk Line as an independent pipeline company. Fortunately for Blair, the government had also directed Trunk Line to operate as a free capitalist enterprise.

As Blair, in his habitual tone of low-key confidence, described the virtues of the project, an occasional eyebrow could be noticed rising. Lanky, soft-spoken Strom's lifelong specialty was not oil but dryland grain farming in the flat plains country of southeastern Alberta. Patrick tended to rely on the advice of his long-serving deputy minister and Govier's expertise. Gerhart would consider any constitutional issues that the project raised. Besides, there were sound reasons for suspecting that Blair, who had only recently switched from the presidency of an American subsidiary to the vice-presidency of an entirely independent Canadian company, was secretly revelling in his new-found freedom of action.

As the meeting drew to an inconclusive close, Premier Strom suggested that Blair send him a written statement of the advantages to Alberta of Trunk Line's involvement in an Arctic gas pipeline. Blair lost no time in doing so, for his freedom was far from absolute: the Trunk Line legislation authorized it to operate only within Alberta, not beyond. So as to be sure that the Trunk North study project would go ahead, Blair wanted Alberta government approval for such an expansion of Alberta Gas Trunk Line's authorized activities.

Blair sent his letter off to Strom on May 19. The letter summarized the advantages to Alberta of the Trunk North Project which had already been discussed at greater length in a report prepared by Trunk Line executive Robin Abercrombie and presented to the government earlier that May. It began by saying that Trunk Line was "reasonably pleased" with results to date in its technical studies and negotiations with potential suppliers and users of northern gas. Blair then noted that encouraging progress had been made towards one of his central purposes for the project, "the important goal of obtaining and protecting a satisfactory position for the Alberta gas transport systems within the over-all development of the gas pipeline artery to be routed through western Canada from Alaska."

Blair made it clear in his letter that his will to carry the project forward required no spiritual sustenance from the government. Strom was told that Trunk Line was anxious to keep his government well informed as the plan proceeded, but Blair said: "We fully accept the responsibility for the commercial challenge in this high stakes negotiating situation."

Blair had no doubt that the proposed Arctic pipeline would be "the future main North American artery for natural gas transport." There would be advantages to the province in keeping it close to Alberta centres of population and industry, despite Alberta's existing huge reserves of fuels, especially in the very long term. "There are economies of scale connected with access to very large gas throughputs," Blair rationalized, "which are advantageous even when there is also sufficient supply available from local fields." A main line like the one proposed would also expedite local field development and off-line local supply in all the areas through which it passed, particularly northern Alberta:

> If the route of the first main passes centrally through Alberta, the Government and private citizens and companies in this province will be involved to a great extent and their public and private policies and investment desires will be reflected in the Alberta portion and throughout the entire development. Conversely, if the route passes by Alberta or crosses only a remote corner, the participation and voice of Alberta interests in the over-all development would probably be negligible.

Even at that early stage in the pipeline planning, Blair had concluded, he informed the Premier that only project sponsorship by Trunk Line was likely to result in a route centrally through Alberta. Other proposed routes would either bypass Alberta altogether or cross only remote parts of its northeastern corner.

Blair's letter included seven pages listing the advantages to Alberta of his proposed project. Gas pipelines and compressor stations with a value of some $300 million would be required in Alberta in the first round of construction then proposed. The value could later double from a northern gas pipeline passing centrally through the province. Large gas storage, processing and liquid extraction operations would also be necessary. New pipe rolling mills, fabricating and assembly installations would be located according to the gas project route. Moreover, the gas artery might well be followed by a major northern oil artery, and a western basic steel industry was possible. Blair argued:

> All this will cause employment during the construction periods and will broaden the tax and industrial base in the province afterward. For instance, the first round of gas pipeline construction mentioned above would alone roughly double the $2 million per year which our company pays currently in taxes to local authorities and would also provide direct employment in operations to several hundreds of Albertans.

The letter ended on a note that gradually grew stronger as the Trunk Line president's arguments evolved. That its tone harked back to Blair's unhappy experiences as president of an American subsidiary seems obvious. The final heading in the letter was "Example of Leadership from Alberta." It might as easily have read "example of leadership from Canada."

"With so much of the capital investment in resource development being produced according to concepts and plans designed in distant headquarters," Blair wrote, with perhaps diplomatic obliqueness, "it must also be healthy to local morale and ambitions to mix in some leadership of large projects by local management, when such opportunity does exist. There are real qualitative values," Blair concluded, "in the example of a $1½ billion enterprise [as Trunk North then modestly envisaged its proposal] in this markedly competitive field being conceived and run from within Alberta."

Blair's letter to Strom further stimulated an already lively in-depth debate among high-ranking Alberta government officials. The reaction of chairman Govier of the Conservation Board and board member Vernon Millard, initially at least, seemed mixed. In one communication they jointly sent to Strom after Blair's letter was circulated among them, they said: "There is no question that substantial real benefits would accrue to Alberta if the project were to proceed, although some of the listed advantages have to be considered speculative. A few fall into the class of the romantic." Which of Blair's claimed advantages fell into the romantic class never seems to have been clearly specified.

The main worries of Alberta's energy officials about the Trunk North Project centred around the possibility that carrying out-of-province gas across Alberta to out-of-province markets could lead to the loss of provincial jurisdiction over Alberta Gas Trunk Line to federal authority. Constitutionally, Ottawa had the last word over interprovincial and international trade. This raised a further fear, one that apparently had been secretly entertained in Edmonton ever since the Alberta Gas Resources Preservation Act had been passed in 1956. If jurisdiction over Trunk Line operations did shift from provincial to federal authority, this might precipitate a challenge to the Gas Resources Preservation Act, which might be found by the courts to be in *ultra vires* of provincial power and thus might lead to loss of provincial control over development, distribution and pricing of Alberta gas, even to Alberta consumers.

Blair found it hard to take such arguments seriously. His response was that the main new element in the Trunk North proposal was the shipment across Alberta of gas produced elsewhere. He mildly noted that this element was apparently not considered important enough to deserve statutory restriction in the legislation establishing Alberta Gas Trunk Line in 1954.

Despite their jurisdictional reservations, Govier (soon to succeed Sommerville as Alberta's deputy energy minister) and other officials quickly came around. They needed little convincing that the potential advantages outweighed the potential disadvantages for Alberta.

Two more important meetings were held during May 1970, one in Cleveland and the other in Chicago. Participants in these meetings included representatives of the Northwest Project Group — which, like the Trunk North Project, had not yet made a public announcement of its plans. Blair still entertained some faint hope that both projects could be merged into a single one. However, his insistence on majority Canadian ownership and control for the Canadian sections of the line, instead of by an American-dominated international consortium, and on the role of common carrier, instead of pipelines controlled by major northern suppliers and customers in the south, proved to be too much of an obstacle. The dominant multinationals are accustomed, the past record makes clear, to exercising all useful ownership and control — and especially control — themselves.

While the earlier meeting in April 1970 with TransCanada had left open some future hope, the meetings in Cleveland and Chicago with the Northwest Project group ended in an atmosphere of finality. "Those meetings," Blair recalled, "concluded with our being told no."

Early in June 1970, Govier and Blair got together and worked out a modification of the initial Trunk North Project concept, at the request of Premier Strom. The solution was simple enough. Alberta Gas Trunk Line would establish a federally chartered, independent, Canadian-owned company to carry northern gas across the Yukon and Northwest Territories to the Alberta border. Trunk Line would then carry it across Alberta to existing pipelines which were already feeding customers in British Columbia, eastern Canada and the United States.

Govier advised Strom, in a June 23 letter representing both his and Blair's agreed views, that the proposed modification did not provide "an absolute guarantee" that Alberta's jurisdiction would be maintained (although to date it has been). But "some increase in the risk of jurisdiction" was warranted by "the undoubted advantages of the project to Alberta."

This letter cleared the way for Blair to make a public announcement on 27 June 1970 of the Trunk North Project, which he and other Alberta Gas Trunk Line executives had been so busily pursuing all over the continent since the beginning of the year. A few days later, after Strom had discussed the project with his cabinet, the Alberta government announced that it was "delighted" about Blair's plans. "Some general advantages which the Government sees" in the project were listed; they were all drawn from Trunk Line communications.

The Alberta government statement, issued by Patrick, mentioned that Trunk Line operated under Alberta regulatory policies, but made a point of noting that the company "is in no way an agency of the Alberta Government." Blair emphasized the same point in the initial presentation of his project before the U.S. Federal Power Commission in Washington on 12 August 1970. He pointed out that Alberta Gas Trunk Line had been established as a private-ownership company, not as a crown corporation or an agency of the Alberta government. Although Trunk Line had operated independently from its inception, Blair kept Edmonton fully informed of the hectic round of negotiations which he and other company executives carried on during the early months of 1970.

The public announcement of the Northwest Project Study Group was made by TransCanada in Toronto on 15 July 1970, some two weeks after Blair's Trunk North Project announcement in Calgary.

(A third group, Mountain Pacific Pipeline Limited, had announced plans for a gas pipeline to Prudhoe Bay more than a year earlier, on 23 June 1969. But the initial intention of this group, with Bechtel Corporation of San Francisco as the American partner, was to connect the British Columbia pipeline system of the Canadian partner, Westcoast Transmission, with new fields expected to be developed in the Fort Liard area of the Northwest Territories, just north of the eastern corner of British Columbia. This group later became dormant. The Mountain Pacific proposal later was negotiated into the Foothills Pipe Lines (Yukon) application, which in turn became part of the Alaska Highway Project.

Within a few days of the 27 June 1970 announcement of its existence, Trunk North hired as a communications consultant Patricia (Pat) Carney, a Vancouver woman journalist with a strong background in economics, and considerable reporting experience in the North. Company files show that, prior to the June announcement, Alberta Gas Trunk Line executives, including Blair, senior vice president W. J. Deyell and vice-president Robin Abercrombie, had discussed how Northerners might be encouraged to participate in the pipeline planning. Thought was also being given to a program for training Northerners both to work on construction of the pipeline and as operators of it afterward. The hiring of Pat Carney rapidly helped to crystallize these plans; in her 31 July 1970 conceptual outline, she wrote:

The proposal to construct a northern natural gas pipeline must deal with certain unusual and highly sensitive factors not normally encountered in conventional pipeline projects. The size and environmental regime pose special engineering and construction problems. Similarly, the economic, sociological, and ecological features will be given unprecedented weight in determining the success of any license application. These unique problems demand unique solutions.

One of the solutions that Trunk North devised was a plan for flying visits by a team of executives and advisers to Northern communities along the proposed pipeline route. Their purpose was twofold: they wanted to explain why the pipeline was being planned, and to inquire of the Northerners they met, whether Indians, Eskimos or whites, what they thought of such a plan. Although the Trunk North planners were undoubtedly motivated in part by their knowledge about the obstacles which were being raised against the Alyeska oil pipeline in Alaska, there were other reasons. One was an understandable sensitivity to the new power of ecology politics. Another was the fact that they were planning to build a pipeline through populated areas in the Mackenzie Valley.

Pat Carney said that this was the first time any resource development company had attemped a "participatory planning" process, one which gave the local inhabitants of a development area an opportunity to have some input into the developers' proposal. Since then, this element has been included in development planning almost routinely.

Another solution that Trunk North came up with that summer of 1970 was a comprehensive program for training Northerners in pipeline skills. Pat Carney recommended an approach that would "contribute to the development of a new Arctic industrial technology which would greatly enhance the level of Canadian expertise," and that would also recognize "the opportunity to integrate many phases of pipeline activity with the special social and economic needs of the North." Not all of Trunk North's motivation for this approach, however, was sheer loving kindness towards Northerners. As Ms. Carney pointed out, "Such corporate emphasis on developing Canadian skills and ability and overall technological capacity is very much in line with stated government policy."

On 12 October 1970, the seven-member Trunk North participatory planning road show took off from Edmonton for a six-day tour along the Mackenzie River to eight communities: Aklavik, Fort McPherson, Fort Good Hope, Norman Wells, Wrigley, Fort Simpson, Inuvik and Yellowknife.

By the time of the tour over the tundra, the Trunk North group had worked out a training program plan to tell the Northerners about. The little groups of residents who turned out in each community were told they would be eligible to participate. Interviewing and recruiting would begin later in 1970, in liaison with representatives of the federal and territorial governments. The trainees would be brought south to Alberta to work on Alberta Gas Trunk Line facilities and learn on the job. They would become permanent employees of Trunk Line, with the option of remaining in the south if they came to prefer life there. After initial orientation, the trainee would have the right to choose his vocation. A Northerner who could relate to the trainees would be assigned to oversee the new recruits.

In each community, three Trunk Line vice-presidents, with Abercrombie as chairman, discussed various aspects of the proposed pipeline. Community representatives were invited to fly over areas adjacent to their communities with Trunk North officials, who pointed out where they proposed to build the pipeline. The local residents were asked to point out their hunting and fishing grounds, and to speak up if the pipeline's suggested location would interfere with their traditional pursuits. The Trunk North team left each community with a promise to return the following May for further dialogue.

A short time later, Northwest Territories Commissioner Stuart M. Hodgson commended Trunk North for its effort to communicate its intentions to the Northerners, but he also passed on the information that the native peoples who had attended the meetings had no idea what natural gas is. He suggested to Pat Carney an analogy the native peoples could readily understand: natural gas was like broken wind — you could hear it, you could smell it, you might even be able to feel it pass, but you could not see it.

On their next visit, in May 1971, the Trunk North tundra travellers took with them models of a river-crossing section of pipeline, a drilling rig and a section of a pipeline buried and above ground on a gravel pad, or berm. The models were hooked to a burner using propane gas. The pipeline and then the gas were explained. The burner was turned on. The Northerners could hear the gas escaping, they could feel its movement with their fingers, and they could smell it. But they could not see it. They understood, usually with a murmured collective "ohhh!" as a match was struck to flame the gas emitted from the burner.

That autumn some native people from Old Crow, believed to be a holy place and the most ancient community in the Yukon, were taken to Rocky Mountain House in Alberta for a demonstration. The plastic model pipeline turned out to be worn a little. When the match was lit, there was a small explosion. A leak caused the models to blow up. No harm was done, except to Trunk North's cause.

There was more dialogue and feedback from the second visit than the first, especially with the native peoples. The Northerners' attitude to the pipeline still seemed wary and sceptical, but expectations were beginning to build up in them. Further visits were made to the communities by individual representatives of the Trunk North Group, and a final group tour was planned. Pat Carney believed this third tour might have convinced Northerners that the pipeliners were really serious about wanting to try to help the North's economy, while helping themselves and other southern interests. The amalgamation of the two groups in 1972 conspired to quash that plan — and in fact to permanently reduce the whole level of socio-economic planning for an Arctic gas pipeline.

3

UNEASY UNION

On 13 August 1970 the federal Minister of Energy, Mines and Resources, J. J. (Joe) Greene, and the Minister of Indian Affairs and Northern Development, Jean Chretien, issued federal government guidelines ''for construction and operation of northern oil and gas pipelines.'' Their news release summarized requirements ''ranging from environment protection, pollution control and Canadian ownership and participation to training and employment of residents of the North.''

The federal guidelines also provided that any Arctic pipeline ''will provide either 'common' carrier service at published tariffs or a 'contract' carrier service at a negotiated price for all oil and gas which may be tendered thereto.''

Two other provisions were of special interest:

1. Means by which Canadians will have a substantial opportunity for participating in the financing, engineering, construction, ownership and management of northern pipelines will form an important element in Canadian Government consideration of proposals for such pipelines.

2. Any applicant must undertake to provide specific programs leading to employment of residents of the North, both during the construction phase and for the operation of the pipeline. For this purpose, the pipeline company will provide for the necessary training of local residents in coordination with various government programs, including on-the-job training projects. The

provision of adequate housing and counselling services will also be a requirement.

Four days after the government's announcement, Robert Blair wrote a letter to Greene saying that he was looking forward to reading the guidelines as soon as he obtained a copy. But he had another matter on his mind. He had noticed in the news media during the last few days a concentration of reports attributing to government spokesmen "a questioning and somewhat critical attitude as to the merits of control by Canadians, through ownership of common equity," of Canadian portions of proposed northern pipelines. Blair told Greene that he found such reports "puzzling." As Greene knew, Alberta Gas Trunk Line's proposed pipeline had as "an express and distinctive feature" the provision that the Canadian segment "shall be owned as to equity by Canadian companies and persons."

Blair went on to explain:

> We built this feature in from the start because of deep conviction that Canadian ownership control of this future gas transport artery would be in the best interests of the Canadian petroleum industry, the western Canadian economy and of Canada. This conviction is in part the result of business experience, to the conclusion that control of a principle pipeline artery by regulatory procedures is *not*, by any means, a fully satisfactory substitute, in terms of developing our industries, for local control and management during the operating period.

A familiar flavour of what some call nationalism, but others may identify as independence, then appeared in Blair's letter.

> The conviction that Canadian control would be desirable also arose from our awareness that in the case of the gas pipeline we had here the business opportunity, for the first time, to construct a major pipeline artery under the leadership of the Canadian management, engineering, financing, and scientific community. This time, at long last, we could set up a project and lead it ourselves, completing the development of skills and reputations that could lead to future international demand, rather than have many key elements of the leadership supplied from outside Canada.

Blair also reviewed for Greene the steps which his company had taken to substantiate "the realism of our intention of Canadian equity ownership.'' The Alberta Gas Trunk Line team had met with Prudhoe Bay producers and the largest prospective customers in the U.S. They had also consulted Canadian underwriters and New York financiers. They were convinced that financing the Canadian sections of the Arctic gas pipeline was "not at all beyond our powers.''

Blair told Greene that he could not fathom any reason for the Canadian government to oppose Canadian equity control of the proposed pipeline. If what he had been reading in the news media meant that cabinet ministers were simply raising questions, then Greene "may feel justly that I have jumped at shadows." But, Blair said somewhat wistfully: "Whether we would soon find another opportunity to lead a project of this scale would be speculative.''

Near the end of his letter, Blair asked two questions for which he offered no answers: "Is it conceivable that others who are interested in corporate control of this artery from the United States are selling a story that there is not sufficient equity financing capability in Canada? Or that this investment is not a suitable one for Canadians?''

Greene's response was sympathetic, but non-committal. The exact form of ownership and control of northern pipelines would not be known until a major government study on foreign ownership in the economy at large was completed, but "certainly, the thinking in Canada today is in the direction of maximum encouragement to projects which produce predominant equity ownership by Canadian companies and individuals.''

Another provision in the Canadian government guidelines stated that, initially, only one trunk gas pipeline would be permitted to be built in the North. The guidelines further said that pipelines would have to be built within a corridor that would be established in consultation with industry and other interested groups.

The incentive and government pressure for the two competing study groups to find some way of getting together was becoming almost irresistible. In addition, the rapid expansion of Blair's Trunk North group ensured that the powerful corporations in the Northwest Group would have to take his threat to their interests seriously.

On 11 December 1970, Blair announced that three U.S. gas transmission companies had joined Trunk Line in an Arctic gas study group. The most important one was the Columbia Gas System, Incorporated, of Wilmington, Delaware, the largest interconnected system in the U.S.; Columbia's subsidiary companies then supplied more than four million customers in seven states from the eastern seaboard to western Ohio. The other new partners were the Northern Natural Gas Company of Omaha, Nebraska, which operates a 26,000-mile transmission and distribution system serving 1,100 communities in the northern plains of the U.S., and Texas Eastern Transmission Corporation of Houston, a major supplier of energy throughout the United States, with a gas system of some 8,500 miles of pipelines, and the only pipeline company serving markets on both the east and west coasts. In March 1971, Blair announced that Canadian National Railways had joined Alberta Gas Trunk Line in a study of the Mackenzie basin as a transportation corridor. The name of the Blair project had gradually evolved from Trunk North to Gas Arctic Systems Study Group.

Despite growing pressure to merge, both the Blair group and the Horte group during 1970 and 1971 busily pursued their separate feasibility studies, negotiations for gas production, sales and delivery arrangements, and otherwise jockeyed for position against the time when formal application to build an Arctic gas pipeline would be made to the Canadian and American governments.

Towards Union
On 3 September 1971, Blair's Arctic Systems Group announced an addition to its membership, Pacific Lighting Gas Development Company, a member of the Pacific Lighting System of Los Angeles. Only the day before, Pacific Development had announced plans for a gas exploration program in the Canadian Arctic islands. By then, Blair's group was also engaged in field surveys and engineering studies pertaining to gathering and transmitting gas from the Arctic islands. Blair welcomed this additional muscle for his group, the more so as negotiations had already been going on for a month toward eventual union with the Northwest Project Group.

Three basic differences had to be resolved between the two competing groups before a merger could be accomplished; these issues concerned financing, common carrier, and ownership. From the beginning, Horte and others in the Northwest Group had shown less optimism or interest than Blair in Canada's capacity to finance, without foreign equity participation, the Canadian section of any Arctic gas pipeline. On this point, the initial July 1970 statement of Northwest said: "It seems clear that, in order to obtain the tremendous amounts of capital that will be required, it will be necessary to obtain firm commitments from large, financially responsible participants to contribute equity capital from time to time to finance construction of the project." Blair had no doubt that Horte had always sincerely believed that Canadian companies alone could not finance the Canadian section of any gas pipeline south from the Arctic. From the viewpoint of Blair and others who had been involved in this project from an early stage, the approach to ownership held by Northwest also smacked of Exxon-dominated tactics — tactics intended to extend its influence and, better still, effective control into any new petroleum field in the world.

The original July 1970 statement of the Northwest Group was not very precise on the question of Canadian ownership of the Canadian section of its proposed pipeline: "Ownership participation in the Canadian portion of the line will be made available to Canadian interests," the statement said, without offering further elaboration. It also indicated that equity ownership in the Canadian sections of any line Northwest built would be wide open to American companies — since the statement was made at a time when the Northwest Group's membership comprised three American gas producers in Alaska, two pipeline companies from the U.S. midwest and only one Canadian pipeline company. The Trunk Line statement concerning the degree of Canadian participation it intended there should be in the ownership of the pipeline it proposed was much clearer. Blair was quoted as saying:

> . . . the equity in the Canadian portion of the pipeline would be held by Canadian investors. Under the terms of the proposal, equity ownership would remain under Canadian control. Debt financing would be raised primarily in the U.S. capital markets, secured in the normal manner by tariff commitments obtained from United States utility companies interested in using the transport system to ship gas south.

Blair believed that the pipeline should be a common carrier. However, the Northwest Group planned to include among any future owners of an Arctic gas pipeline both producers at one end and customers at the other. The Northwest statement said that its pipeline "would transport gas for sellers and purchasers of gas without regard to ownership interests in the line." It also promised that "other producers and pipeline interests will be invited to participate in the ownership of the facilities." These vague promises were not enough to dissuade Blair from what he had told Horte in their April 1970 meeting: if the Arctic gas pipeline was to maintain complete autonomy to act as a neutral and common carrier, ownership of the company should not include any shipper.

The initial contact towards an amalgamation of their two groups was made by Horte and Blair on 5 August 1971. At that time Horte was still president of TransCanada PipeLines. They arranged a larger meeting of representatives of the Arctic Systems and Northwest Groups on 27 August 1971 in Toronto's Royal York Hotel.

On August 14, Blair sent a telex to Horte about that meeting. Assuming there was a successful marriage of their separate projects, Blair said that TransCanada and Trunk Line should "work in concert with each other" as well as within the joined study groups to develop alternative approaches for moving Arctic gas through southern Canada. These alternatives would include "moving initial quantities [of gas] by looping expansions of our existing system and your existing system." Blair's telex also suggested that provision should be made in plans for the amalgamated project to move "a portion of future Arctic gas supply to western markets." At that point, the major American companies serving the natural gas needs of the western United States, in particular California, were either in Blair's group or the Mountain Group organized by Westcoast Transmission. The Northwest Group was dominated by companies more interested in eastern markets in Canada and the United States.

During the next several months, Northwest and Arctic Systems carried on their amalgamation negotiations at meetings in Houston, Denver, Omaha, Calgary, Toronto and Chicago. At a meeting of the Arctic Systems Group's executive committee in Calgary on 21 December 1971, Blair reported that a meeting with the Northwest Group in Chicago had been "a courteous and friendly meeting." At that point, there was a difference of some $1.2 billion between Arctic Systems' lower estimate of the cost of building a gas pipeline south across Canada from the Arctic and the Northwest Group's $4 billion estimate. It had been agreed that those responsible for the conflicting estimates would meet in Calgary to iron out the difference.

At the same Chicago meeting, the minutes show that Harry L. Lepape, president of Pacific Lighting Gas Development in Los Angeles and a member of the Arctic Systems Group, "expressed his company's great concern" that feasibility studies for the Northwest Group so far had been concentrated "on the basis of all gas going to eastern markets." Negotiating for a merger with Northwest on the basis of that plan "would not be in the best interest of his company." The meeting was then advised that two Arctic Systems' studies were nearly completed, one on sending 25 per cent of the Arctic gas west and the other on sending 50 per cent west. Lepape was urged to make sure that his company was represented at the next meeting of the two groups to pursue this interest.

In the early months of planning of both groups, Blair continued to hope that he could interest Horte in his plan, which was essentially to use or expand existing pipelines in southern Canada to handle Arctic gas. Thus a new pipeline, along new right-of-way, would need to be built only from the Arctic south to the northernmost terminus of the existing lines. Blair foresaw this providing new expansion not only for his Alberta Gas Trunk Line, but for Westcoast Transmission's system in British Columbia, and for Horte's TransCanada PipeLines across Saskatchewan and Manitoba.

In Blair's notes of his April 1970 meeting with Horte, he still seemed to believe there was some chance of TransCanada going along with Trunk Line. Blair recorded that Horte "emphasized that their position in another gas pipeline project [Northwest] can only be considered as preliminary in nature and an attempt to get some feel as to the economics of transporting gas from the northern areas." Fourteen months later, Blair's hopes on this score had begun to wane.

Minutes of an Arctic Systems policy committee meeting in Calgary on 23 June 1971 recorded that Dr. Robert A. Bandeen of Toronto, then vice-president of Canadian National Railways (and incidentally Blair's brother-in-law), advised the meeting that TransCanada "appears most anxious to join the undertaking." Trunk Line vice-president Gordon Walker indicated that TransCanada "might wish to get in on the Arctic Gas portion of it [from the Mackenzie Delta] and not the Prudhoe Bay part.'' The minutes then recorded, however, that Blair's hopes about TransCanada had turned to suspicions. ''Mr. Blair advised the meeting that he wishes TransCanada in the undertaking, but there are problems, for TransCanada has considered itself to be the leader in the Northwest Group and TransCanada might intend to take over the undertaking.''

On 1 February 1972 Horte headed a four-member delegation from the Northwest Group at a meeting in Toronto's Royal York Hotel with a three-man delegation from Arctic Systems led by Blair. Horte's delegation included W. R. (Ray) Booth of Houston, representing Exxon through its subsidiary Humble Oil. The minutes of that meeting tersely recorded some difference between the two groups over proposed voting procedure for the amalgamation of their groups. The Northwest group, the minutes noted, ''felt their proposed voting procedure would give adequate protection to the Canadian transporters position.'' The Arctic Systems group dissented; they ''felt that the proposed voting procedure may be unwieldy and would not satisfy the Canadian transporters position if the study group were to control the initial applicant company.''

At that meeting the Arctic Systems group also set out certain studies and terms of reference that it thought should be part of any merger agreement:

— Studies should include provision for piping Arctic gas to markets in the western United States. Northwest, the minutes say, ''agreed this was necessary as well as desirable.''

— There should be no strategy preference for an ''express'' line oriented to the eastern market and excluding Alberta Gas Trunk Line ownership of the part in Alberta. There should be ''a clear field'' for Trunk Line ''to present its case'' for a Trunk Line-TransCanada oriented facility to serve the east and west. Northwest, the minutes said, ''stated they could accept this premise provided that suitable language could be developed.''

— The system would be a ''neutral'' contract carrier ''serving new customers as well as original, as long as service to original customers was not therefore made deficient.'' To this, the minutes said that Northwest agreed.

— Off-line sales would be provided to Canadian customers along the route. Northwest agreed.

— On a discussion of Canadian-ownership principles during this meeting, the minutes recorded:

Both parties seemed agreed on the principle of maximum Canadian control and ownership of the Canadian portion of the line, although Northwest wanted Canadian financibility established before yielding control from the study group, while Blair felt that it was essential for Canadian companies to control the Canadian application from the start. Blair felt confident of the ability of Canadians to finance their share of the project and therefore this was really not an issue in his mind. He suggested that a minority fraction of the Canadian portion could be reserved for the other interested parties (suppliers and purchasers). However, the control would be firmly in the hands of the Canadian transporters.

The Northwest position, as described here, was significant. It meant that the Northwest Group — its chairman then was W. H. (Deke) Mack of Detroit, president of Michigan Wisconsin Pipe Line — was unwilling to agree unconditionally to allow a company owned and controlled by Canadians to apply for the right to build the Canadian section or sections of an Arctic gas pipeline. The Northwest Group, then dominated by foreign-controlled companies, wanted to maintain the right to apply for Canadian pipeline rights for itself, unless and until a Canadian-controlled company could prove that it was capable of financing this huge project. The questions were: How would "financibility" be measured? And by whom?

Would the large American companies interested in the project — those with gas in Alaska to sell, along with those wanting to distribute the gas to their customers in the south 48 states — be prepared to put up the mortgage or debt capital, or some of it? Since all the money required could not be raised in Canada, large proportions of it would have to be raised through the sale of bonds abroad. This was the usual way of financing a pipeline. The equity investment — the investment that gave ownership and control — would be only a minority part of the financing, and it might well be financible in Canada, provided the debt financing could be arranged abroad.

The Northwest "financibility" condition thus provided it with a loophole with a variety of potential uses, all with control as an end.

A report of the Toronto meeting noted that it appeared as though the Northwest Group might swing closer to the concepts of Arctic Systems, provided that suitable language could be developed on the key points of Alberta Gas Trunk Line's special position and the concept of Canadian control of the Canadian application and ownership of the Canadian section. From Blair's viewpoint, this soon proved to have been an overly optimistic expectation.

Agreement appeared to have been reached during that meeting on another difference in approach of special interest to Blair and Trunk Line, the ownership of different sections of the pipeline. The Northwest Group wanted Arctic gas to move south in a pipeline across Canada owned by a single company, not through a line in which different sections would be owned by different companies. Because of the different government jurisdictions it would pass through, the complexity of financing, and so on, Horte later told me "there was a feeling that it would be a mistake to have divided ownership. It would be much simpler to have one line." Blair disagreed. He wanted the section of the line across the Yukon and Northwest Territories to be owned by a new company, and the rest of the line ownership divided between Trunk Line and Trans-Canada (Westcoast Transmission came into the picture later.) The minutes said: "While the Northwest Group's opening position was for a single-ownership line from Prudhoe Bay to Emerson [on the Canadian-U.S. border in Manitoba], they finally conceded that they could agree to a system owned by a number of companies, each with a different share structure and control." On this point, too, the minutes later proved to have been overly optimistic.

The Toronto meeting ended with a decision to leave further merger discussions "subject to arrangements by Horte and Blair." A flurry of individual contacts then developed, especially among American members of both groups; the initiative came from the Northwest Group.

These contacts were discussed during a meeting of the Arctic Systems Group's executive committee at the Hyatt House hotel at the Seattle-Tacoma airport on 16 February 1972. The total communication (verbal and written) from Northwest, a report said, seemed to be somewhat mixed. Blair was asked to telephone Horte during the meeting for some technical clarifications, which he did, and the report said that there was agreement that merger with Northwest was still desirable in spite of apparent current difficulties in achieving this. Arctic Systems members were assigned to follow up the recent contacts with Northwest members for "further verbal clarification of the position of individual members."

A crucial meeting of the two groups was held in Chicago on

April 5 and 6. Blair led a delegation of fifteen, eight of them representatives of American companies participating in his group. There were nine in the Northwest Group delegation, including Horte, but the major influence on Northwest's side during that meeting was Deke Mack.

The meeting had no formal structure, and opened with a brief oral review of negotiations to date and a general agreement to concentrate on eliminating differences. Blair spoke early in the meeting, stressing the importance "in the Canadian political context, of the initial Canadian application being controlled by Canadians, even though such application was under the necessary overall guidance of the study group." By then the American representatives knew what to expect from Blair, but they were either still not convinced Canadians could finance the Canadian sections of the pipeline themselves, or were unwilling to give up equity participation and perhaps controlling interest in the line themselves.

Blair again spelled out Trunk Line's special interests; it wished to maintain its position as exclusive gatherer of gas within Alberta as set by Alberta Government policy. In a later interview, Horte spoke about the "special nature" of Alberta Gas Trunk Line and indicated that it was a source of some concern, government being involved and all, to some Northwest Group members. Americans attending the Chicago meeting had reason to know how Trunk Line had cut producers in Alberta out of their customary ownership of gathering and other pipelines. Now Blair was proposing a similar arrangement for Arctic gas pipelines across Canada. Blair told the meeting that Trunk Line would not insist on ownership of "through" line facilities that essentially cut across the northeastern corner of the province, but would want to negotiate for ownership of any "through" line facilities that cut through the heart of Alberta.

The issue of single or multiple ownership of the line came up again. "It was noted," the minutes recorded, "that the Alberta portion of pipeline facilities currently delivering gas to California and to eastern Canada and midwest U.S. markets was owned by Alberta Gas Trunk Line and successfully operated in relay with other pipeline companies."

Union Accomplished

A merger agreement was finally executed following a meeting in

Houston on 8 June 1972, with Horte as chairman. The new name agreed upon was Gas Arctic/Northwest Project Study Group. At the last minute, four new participants were accepted into the group, three of them representing three of the "Seven Sisters." The new representatives were Gulf Oil Canada Limited, Imperial Oil Limited (Exxon's Canadian subsidiary), Shell Canada Limited, and Canadian Pacific Investments Limited. Altogether at that meeting there were 41 people (13 Canadian and 28 American) representing 9 American companies, 4 Canadian companies and 3 Canadian subsidiaries of foreign companies. (Two of the companies, Humble and Imperial Oil, were Exxon subsidiaries.) Also present were four study group officials and two lawyers, W. W. Brackett of Chicago representing Northwest and J. L. Lewtas of Toronto representing Arctic Systems.

One of the officials present was Harry E. Palmer of Calgary, secretary of the Arctic Systems executive committee. He took minutes on behalf of Lewtas, who had been appointed permanent secretary of the merged group. In a 12 June 1972 letter to Lewtas, accompanying a draft of the Houston minutes, Palmer commented: "I must say that this was very much like trying to take minutes of a meeting held in a revolving door of Eaton's on $1.49 day!"

The agreement was effective from 1 June 1972. The original signatories were:

Canadian
> TransCanada PipeLines Limited
> Canadian National Realities, Limited
> Canadian Pacific Investments Limited
> The Alberta Gas Trunk Line Company Limited

Foreign-controlled Canadian subsidiaries
> Gulf Oil Canada Limited
> Imperial Oil Limited
> Shell Canada Limited

American
> Atlantic Richfield Company
> Columbia Gas Transmission Corporation
> Michigan Wisconsin Pipe Line Company
> Natural Gas Pipeline Company of America

Northern Natural Gas Company
Pacific Lighting Gas Development Company
The Standard Oil Company of Ohio
Texas Eastern Transmission Corporation
Humble Oil and Refining Company

The emphasis on financibility as a key factor in ownership and control of the eventual pipeline was reinforced in the merger agreement. Robin Abercrombie of the Arctic Systems Group still remembered the direction in which Exxon's interests were usually focused, both during the pre-merger negotiations and the merger. Exxon's representatives were always concentrated on finance and public relations. An interest in finance has long been understandable through the old truism, "He who pays the piper calls the tune." A more modern element of power might need a new verbal conveyance, something like "He who influences the public presentation of a cause, influences the impression it makes on the public."

The studies of both groups in the merger, said the agreement, "each indicate that a pipeline project of the size required for economic transportation of natural gas from northern Alaska and Northwest Canada . . . will involve the expenditure of extremely large sums of money, involving novel financing problems." To anyone familiar with Northwest Group strategy up to then, there was a ring of familiarity about another sentence in the same paragraph, in section 2 on page 2 of the agreement: "The immensity and unique nature of the project indicate that the cooperation and participation of a substantial segment of the natural gas industry will be desirable, and may be essential, to the successful completion of the project." Note that the reference to the "natural gas industry" did not distinguish it by countries: it was not "the Canadian natural gas industry," or "the American natural gas industry" — just "the natural gas industry."

As several Canadians who participated in these meetings, both before and after the merger, told me, the multinational corporate view of the world does not see it divided up into separate countries, but into different industries and economic entities. We may, indeed, one day realize that the multinational corporations were in fact the realistic forerunners of a single united world community. My informants did say that the multinational corporate view, particularly as evinced in their observations of the Exxon participants in this project, is neither conspiratorial nor consciously given to evil intent against humanity as a whole. The multinational mind,

48

without exercising moral judgment of any kind, sees profit — not national or public interest — as the primary purpose of business. It is neither the Canadian way nor the American way nor any other nationalistic way that is best; it is the most efficient — and profitable — way that is best. This is the multinational motivation that unifies the world in the pursuit of profit — and may one day unify humanity on other bases as governments are forced to cope globally with the new forces unleashed, inadvertently or otherwise, by multinational corporate activities. The forces of evolution are never all good.

Blair had always been wary, if not outright suspicious, about the Northwest Group's treatment of the financibility provisions. There was a lot of good sense in the policy. No doubt there would be many "novel financing problems" in putting together the most costly pipeline project ever tried. Certainly "the immensity and unique nature of the project" would require co-operation and participation of "a substantial segment of the natural gas industry." But the most substantial segment by far was in the United States and there were a variety of ways of handling the novel financing problems. Furthermore, the policy lent itself to a convincing public presentation in as wide a variety of ways as it did to handling the financing problems. Blair feared that this flexibility had but one underlying purpose: to keep effective control in multinational hands, more particularly in the hands of Exxon and other American companies, not the least among them Deke Mack's Michigan Wisconsin Pipe Line Company.

Some of Blair's uneasiness over the Canadian-control provisions in the merger agreement was evident in a memo which he sent to Lewtas, the Arctic Systems Toronto lawyer, on 7 April 1972. He drew Lewtas' attention to a statement on Canadian ownership put forward by the Northwest Group for inclusion in the merger agreement: " . . . Canadians will be given the right to invest in the Canadian company to the maximum extent feasible." He found the statement not very specific and explained why it worried him. It "may leave the practical judgment of feasibility in the power of the predominantly U.S. membership of the management committee, who may give much weight to alleged influences upon such feasibility that Canadian public interest would give less weight." Blair continued:

> I still have the apprehension that TransCanada and some of the
> U.S. members might maintain, for instance, that the judgement

of Morgan, Stanley can be cited as establishing the maximum extent of Canadian participation which will be feasible. That could lead to a majority judgment of the Management Committee that only a small percentage was so feasible, and leave the onus of challenging such conclusion on an Alberta Gas Trunk Line-Canadian National minority in the management committee, or upon the Government of Canada or interveners, who would have then to argue against the position of expertise which would be assumed by the applicant.

Eventually the merged Gas Arctic/Northwest Project Study Group appointed the Canadian firm of Wood Gundy Limited of Toronto as its financial advisers, though the American preference was the New York City firm of Morgan Stanley. Indeed, one way or another, Morgan Stanley continued to be perhaps the decisive influence on financial decisions by the Gas Arctic/Northwest Project Study Group, some participants still believe.

The merger agreement included a provision that the new group's feasibility studies would include possible pipeline projects "serving eastern, central and western market areas," a provision initiated by the Blair group. The agreement also covered participation by study group members in the company to be set up, if, as and when an application was made to build the pipeline. Study group participants initially would have "equal undivided interests" in the company, but the question of ultimate ownership could not be decided at that time. It was desirable and appropriate, however, that participants "have some reasonable opportunity to acquire ownership interests" in the company eventually building the pipeline.

When he saw the part in the agreement on Canadian participation, Blair's unease became permanent, though by then he had little choice but to go along with it, as far as he could. The Northwest Group's financibility provision had been written in, complete with legal flourishes. That part read:

. . . with respect to any corporation owning any part of the Project situated within Canada:
(i) Canadians shall be given the opportunity to acquire ownership in the corporation to the maximum extent feasible and consistent with the formulation of a practicable over-all permanent financing plan for the Project; and
(ii) the participants which are Canadian will be given the prior

opportunity to make acquisitions out of that portion of the ownership interest referred to in clause (i) which is offered in accordance with such financing plan to corporate purchasers.

Nowhere was there any mention of majority Canadian equity ownership and control of the Canadian section of any Arctic gas pipeline, as Blair had wanted from the beginning. Clearly, this round went to Horte's side. But whether, as Blair had feared, the project had been taken over by TransCanada PipeLines, was less easy to determine.

Horte insisted that his group had been dominated by its Toronto management all through the long piece. At this Blair and others involved tended to smile and shake their heads or raise an eyebrow. There was no doubt in their minds that Horte's group had been dominated from the beginning by the American partners, with Exxon more dominant than the others — though Deke Mack, the tall, heavily-structured chairman, is credited by Blair and others as possibly the strongest single personality which the group experienced.

The voting procedure which had been put forward earlier by the Northwest Group, the one which Arctic Systems suspected as not providing Canadians with enough power to protect their own interests, was also written into the merger agreement. This procedure divided the participants into three groups: U.S. companies other than producers, Canadian companies other than producers, and Canadian and U.S. producers. Any decision would require a two-thirds approval of participants in each of these groups. Horte said that this provided the Canadian companies with all the power that they would need, a virtual veto on any decision, if they wanted to exercise it. What he did not point out was that it also gave the gas producers, none of which was Canadian-controlled, the same veto power.

One of the times during our interview when Vern Horte's brown eyes flashed with what I took as indignation, or perhaps resentment, or just plain anger, was when he said: "Blair never wanted to join our group. We took the initiative. We negotiated with him for months, and it was finally the U.S. companies in his group that said to him 'join or else' and he had to. It's awfully clear to me," he went on, his eyes flashing again, "that Bob Blair really came into the union in the first instance kicking and screaming."

At that particular moment, Horte was sitting bare-chested on a sofa in his Calgary Inn suite, perspiration pouring off him and a freshly-lit menthol cigarette between his fingers. It was just after 7 a.m. and he had returned from what had obviously been a brisk jog around Prince's Island Park nearby only moments before I arrived for an hour-long breakfast interview. He was on his third cigarette by the time breakfast arrived. When he had cooled down a little, physically, he put the jacket of his blue jogging suit back on.

Horte said that it had been the pressure of the Canadian government guidelines, particularly the provision that only one main trunk pipeline would be approved, that had brought the two groups together.

Blair agreed with Horte on that point. Intercepted during a sunny winter's noon-hour a few days later, in a hall outside his Calgary office on the thirty-seventh floor of Bow Valley Square 2, Blair responded mildly. If anything, his eyes had a twinkle of amusement in them instead of the expected flash of indignation at another mention of Horte. "I think he's exaggerating a bit," Blair said of Horte's comment that Blair had been forced into the union with the Northwest Group by his U.S. partners. "But there's quite a bit of truth in it." Under the pressure of the government guidelines, Trunk Line, said Blair, "accepted terms we otherwise wouldn't have because of pressure from our American partners."

A Time of Indigestion
Harry Palmer, who now works for Dome Petroleum Limited in Calgary, had been secretary to the executive committee of Blair's Gas Arctic Systems Group during the merger meetings. His job was to take notes for the minutes and it required that he pay close attention to everything which everyone said. He told me in an interview that there was no doubt in his mind whatever that the American companies in the Northwest Group had control of it — they had an 80 per cent interest in it, and TransCanada PipeLines had 20 per cent — and intended to maintain control of the merged group as well. "There was no doubt that the U.S. companies wanted to keep control. Their hope was that they would just kind of gobble up Trunk Line in the merger." He chuckled at some of his recollections. "There were some very interesting times at those meetings. Not all of them got into the minutes, either."

One of Blair's chief interests had been to ensure that there was

52

the right wording in the merger agreement to allow his company to pull out, if it found the going too little to its liking. As things turned out, the attempt to gobble up Trunk Line produced mostly indigestion.

The battle of Blair's minority forces had begun even before the merger. During the merger talks, Blair had frequently found himself "butting heads," as one participant put it to me, at executive meetings with Deke Mack.

Mack, now 66 and retired, though still acting as a consultant for Michigan Wisconsin Pipe Line, was born in Westfield, Massachusetts. He graduated from Dartmouth College, the New Hampshire member of the Ivy League, in 1932 and received a law degree from George Washington University in 1935. He lived in posh Detroit suburbia, on Country Club Drive in a community called Grosse Pointe Farms.

One Canadian I spoke to remembers him as "prepossessing." Not only was he taller, at six foot one or two, than most others at any of the meetings, but his body had a big frame. He wore horn-rimmed glasses and dark gray pinstriped suits and exuded a big-business confidence as imposing as his physical presence. He was accustomed to being in charge, and usually was. Several Canadians who saw him in action at many meetings said that he made no effort to conceal his opposition to Trunk Line's Canadian-control ambitions. Sometimes, one told me, Deke Mack just sat there silently shaking his head, as if he could not comprehend this competition for control.

At a management committee meeting in Omaha on 9 May 1972, three co-chairmen were chosen on an interim basis to represent the group (then in the process of merging) before public bodies. They were Vernon Horte, Robert Blair and W. H. (Deke) Mack. At that meeting, Mack had one of his top lieutenants, Karl E. Schmidt of Detroit, senior vice-president of Michigan Wisconsin Pipe Line, named chairman of the influential technical committee. The Exxon delegates, headed by Carl G. Herrington of Houston, vice-president of Humble Oil, successfully put forward L. R. Moore of Humble as chairman of the key finance committee. The chairmanship of the public affairs committee went to R. M. Donaldson of Cleveland, one of the Standard Oil (Sohio) men.

A month later, during the actual merger meeting in Houston's Sonesta Hotel, Horte informed the large gathering of corporate delegates of a letter he had received from the new Canadian

Minister of Energy, Mines and Resources, Donald Macdonald. By all accounts, Mack was as chagrined as anyone at the meeting to learn that Canadian government policy demanded that Canadian-owned engineering firms be given the lead role in Canadian aspects of this project. This precipitated one of the first in a long line of Blair-Mack confrontations.

The problem arose out of the fact that Williams Brothers Canada Limited were the Northwest Group's construction consultants, and this Calgary-based company was controlled from an American parent company in Tulsa. Horte advised the same meeting that the Williams Brothers contract was up for renewal on July 1. Mack, especially, wanted the contract renewed, but Blair reminded him that this would not be agreeable to the Canadian government. Eventually it was decided that the three co-chairmen should arrange to meet with Donald Macdonald, and that Williams Brothers should become "Canadianized" in its ownership.

Horte, Mack and Blair met Macdonald in Ottawa on 28 June 1972. Horte later wrote up meeting notes agreed upon by the other two co-chairmen. On the Williams Brothers issue, Horte reported:

> Considerable discussion took place with respect to the use of U.S. and Canadian consultants.
> (a) The Government's basic plan is that the expertise in connection with northern pipelines be developed in Canada, so that in future Canadian firms would be looked to as the experts with respect to northern pipelines and would be able to do the job that we now indicate Williams Brothers is capable of doing.
> (b) He accepts that Williams Brothers must be involved, but stated that they must not be the dominant engineering firm or in a position that appears dominant.
> (c) The Minister has a political problem which we must recognize. In answer to a direct question, he indicated that some new firm, or consortium, that was not dominated by Williams Brothers may be the answer.

In the course of the engineering company issue, a man named Gordon Walker found himself swept right out of the project. A big man with crewcut dark hair, and a manner sometimes as burly as his build, Walker had moved from vice-president engineering with Trunk Line to supervise engineering studies for Arctic Systems. After the merger, he became — for a while — director of engineering of the new Canadian Arctic Gas Study Group Limited

(CAGSL). (By then, the merged group had adapted a version of the name used by Blair's Gas Arctic Systems Group to describe itself, and planned to put forward a pipeline application in the name of the company it established for that purpose, Canadian Arctic Gas Pipeline Limited. The two names, CAGSL and CAGPL, are interchangeable, but for the sake of simplicity will, from here on, be referred to as Arctic Gas.) At the Houston meeting, Walker had been asked for his recommendations as to what the new group's future relationship with Williams Brothers should be. After considerable wrangling, Mack, Blair, Horte and a few others were sent to another room and assigned to work out a resolution covering the future relationship of Williams Brothers with the new group. At issue was the Canadian government demand that a Canadian firm be given the leadership role. The compromise policy which was finally approved said that the report from Walker had indicated clearly the desirability of continuing at a substantial level of employment of the Williams Brothers firm within the management structure of the combined group. The meeting approved negotiations for a new contract with Williams Brothers.

Following the meeting with Energy Minister Macdonald, a Toronto meeting of the management committee in July 1972 was advised that conversations had already begun between Williams Brothers and a Calgary firm, Pemcan Services (then a consultant to Arctic Systems) which in 1973 became a partner along with Swan Wooster Engineering Company Limited of Vancouver in the Northern Engineering Company.

During the next year, a company was established, Northern Engineering Services Limited, with headquarters in Calgary. Horte told the National Energy Board in April 1977 that Arctic Gas had kept Northern Engineering fully employed as consultants ever since. The staff numbered about 135 when Horte talked to the NEB, but had reached as high as 170. The company was about 75 per cent beneficially owned by Canadians, including Williams Brothers (Canada), which in turn was owned 50-50 by its American parent and Swan Wooster.

Meanwhile, Williams Brothers went ahead with more work for Arctic Gas. Though officially the firm was supposed to report to Walker, he and other Canadians say that it appeared to be reporting to Mack and Horte more often than to Walker. As soon as Northern Engineering came into the picture, Mack had his own representative working within the company. One Canadian told me that an Exxon man informed him during a private conversation that they were determined to see Walker replaced, apparently because Walker was determined that, as director of engineering, he, and not Williams Brothers, would direct the engineering studies. Eventually, Walker did leave.

A main point of contention, Walker said, was his opposition to various engineering studies which he believed were unnecessary and wasteful of the group's spending. Now a private consultant in Calgary, Walker said that his impression was that some of the studies were intended only to make work for Northern Engineering. He cited as an example a proposal for a new design study on how to build a concrete pad for building sites in the North, when a basic engineering design had been worked out long ago and was adaptable anywhere.

By the fall of 1972, a Williams Brothers study had been prepared comparing costs for alternative routes for Arctic Gas pipeline. When it was circulated on 13 October to members of Arctic Gas, Blair was concerned that the report offered no cost analysis of building southern sections of the pipeline along the existing routes of Trunk Line and TransCanada. On October 18, Blair sent a telex to all the other members of the management committee, complaining that:

> The terms of the study group agreement and the definition of the base case as approved by the executive committee call for the consideration of expansion of existing systems as one of the alternatives for transportation of Arctic gas. The Williams Brothers report . . . does not provide information on this alternative. We believe it would be improper and not in accordance with the terms of the study group agreement, to make any route selections until the possibility of expansion of existing systems is fully considered.

The telex advised that Trunk Line and TransCanada were co-operating in a joint study on this point and would make the material available by the end of the month.

By this time William Price Wilder had been chosen chairman and chief executive officer of the group, through a process Blair still recalls, more with wry resignation than bitterness, as a "railroad job." This is not, of course, the way Wilder and others on his side now remember it, and in fact the choice of Wilder was unanimous. Blair says that he accepted the choice only when he saw there was no use opposing it.

Wilder's name had first been put forward by J. A. Armstrong of Imperial Oil as the only man in Canada fit for the job. Blair and other Canadians said that they had a feeling that this had already been planned, with the main influence coming from Mack and Exxon representatives — one of which, of course, was Armstrong, as the chairman of Imperial Oil.

William Price Wilder is a Torontonian, born on 26 September 1922. In his way he is as much an eastern Canada establishment man as Mack is an eastern U.S. establishment man. Wilder was not an oilman, but an investment dealer, having joined Wood Gundy Limited after obtaining a Bachelor of Commerce degree from McGill University in 1946. He took two years off to attend the Harvard graduate school of business, where he earned an MBA in 1950. He was a past president of the Investment Dealers Association of Canada. Wilder had been the president of Wood Gundy since 1967.

Blair had initially opposed Wilder's appointment. "I tried to keep it open," he recalled, "partly because it was such an obvious railroad job." Blair disagreed with Armstrong's insistence that a financier was needed in the job for another reason. "I thought we needed a real lion of a man for this new job — not a technician." A technician, as he considered Wilder to be, would probably turn out to be rather meek, especially in standing up for Canadian interests against American. As far as Blair was concerned, that was how Wilder turned out. Morgan Stanley were financial advisers to Exxon, and Blair also saw Wood Gundy as the closest in style to Morgan Stanley of any financial outfit in Canada.

Horte and Blair had been assigned to draw up a short list of other possible candidates, though Blair still recalled an attitude of impatience from other executive committee members, as though the issue had already been settled. Once, while riding in a taxi with Horte — in what city is forgotten — Blair said that they had asked each other whether either was interested in the job. Both said a firm no. They called on Wilder a few times about the job, and Horte usually stayed behind for a private chat when Blair left. As soon as Wilder had been named chairman, he had put Horte forward, successfully, as president of the new consortium.

An Early Clash For The New Ethic

Part of the baggage which the Arctic Systems Group brought to the merger with Northwest Group was the Environment Protection Board, which had been established initially in September 1970 by Alberta Gas Trunk Line. The board's terms of reference included a promising reflection of the new capitalist development ethic previously referred to. Two of the board's members pointed out the singularity of its position in contemporary industry, in a paper prepared at the height of the merger negotiations.

The paper, prepared by D. W. Clark and Dr. George Calef, both of Winnipeg, pointed out that "the concept of an industrially sponsored Environment Protection Board is new to Canada." The authors emphasized that the most unusual aspect of the board's terms of reference was the independence it was given. The paper said that in the board's initial stages, the focus had been on providing it with "sufficient autonomy and support to carry out its advance investigations and make its recommendations with adequate freedom." The paper, at a later point, indicated that the efforts to ensure the board's independence had been successful — up to then, at least.

The paper went on to say that:

> The Alberta Gas Trunk Line Company recognized that industry did not enjoy a generally healthy reputation about consideration of environmental matters and to some extent about disclosure of information. In view of this the [board] enjoys the right to make its formal reports to the Gas Arctic Systems public without prior editing by the sponsor. This policy is extended to all EPB publications such as newsletters and brochures. This has helped enhance the most important feature of the "board" concept, namely, its autonomous nature. It has allowed the performance of research work and publication of information at the board's discretion.

The paper also pointed out that, as conceived by the Arctic Systems group, the board would continue to monitor the pipeline project throughout the four years of its anticipated construction period, "and for a suitable period during the operational phase" afterwards. "Clearly," the paper announced, in an outburst of excessive optimism, at another point, "we have entered a new era in which technological projects must justify themselves on environmental grounds as well as by the traditional technological and economic considerations.''

The merger meeting of the two groups in Omaha, a report said, supported the overall concept of an independent Environment Protection Board. However, a request was also supported that a review be begun with the board about a revision of their future role. The six terms of reference to be covered in this review included limiting interim disclosures to factual data and withholding interim opinions.

As the merger talks progressed, Environmental Protection Board chairman Carson H. Templeton prepared a short statement describing the philosophy and function of the board for a meeting between the two groups in mid-April 1972. The statement, dated 18 March 1972, made clear the board members felt their role should continue in the merged group on the same basis as had been initially agreed upon with Trunk Line. Under ''philosophy,'' it said:

> The board is a group of environmental experts experienced in Arctic conditions who accept the premise that a gas pipeline from the Arctic to southern Canada *can* be constructed and operated with no more than a reasonable and acceptable degree of alteration to the natural environment.
>
> The board believes that it should conduct its operations to see that the line *will* be constructed and operated in a manner that will minimize the detrimental effects on the environment. It should also recognize the sponsor's need for flexibility in designing and operating the line in an adequate and economic manner.

The statement then moved into the sensitive area of the board's future independence:

> The board has an internal role of advising the sponsor. It also has an external role in the matter of relations with government and conservation groups, as well as the monitoring of construction work, preparation of technical reports and post-construction evaluation. Unless both roles are adequately filled, the ''board approach'' should not be used.

To perform these roles, the statement went on:

1. The board must be autonomous and free to determine what research, in its view, is needed.

2. The board needs to establish its credibility with government and conservationists. A key feature is that its autonomous nature must be demonstrated to outsiders.

3. The board's findings should be made public (after a lead time suitable to permit review by the sponsor) without editing by the sponsor.

The statement gave to the future sponsor the only concession then enjoyed by its existing sponsor: the board would submit budgets and the sponsor would have the right to limit them.

By the time that the management committee of the merged Arctic Gas group met in Toronto on 22 September 1972, Horte, by then the group's president, had a report to present on the review of the Environment Protection Board's terms of reference thereafter. Horte's report noted that under its original arrangement with Blair's group, the EPB "was given full authority in connection with all environmental studies." Arctic Systems controlled the board's budget, "but having done so they could not exercise control over what studies would be done." Horte also noted that the "EPB was to have an on-going function, not only during the construction phase but also after operations had begun."

Horte advised that, in future, the board continue to "recommend" environmental programs to the merged group, as would its own retained environmentalists. "But we will, following such advice, determine and decide which studies will be undertaken and by whom these studies will be conducted." The Arctic Gas group would be prepared to make all its information available to the board on pipeline routes and hear its advice, but "we will make the decisions as to routing." Nor would the board any longer have responsibility for preparing the group's environmental impact statement. Said Horte's report: "The environmental impact statement will be prepared by us." Post-construction monitoring of the pipeline's impact on the environment was also out.

The hope was expressed in Horte's report that future interim reports by the board would "not be issued without a thorough review by us." They should also "avoid raising questions on the environmental matters when in fact the results of studies in connection with those matters are not yet known." Horte hoped that "something along these lines" could be worked out with the board. However, "in the event that they believe they must have full control over the environmental aspects of the project, it would be our recommendation that we would then have to terminate our arrangements.''

A report of the Toronto meeting stated that, after discussion, the proposals in Horte's report were approved. The shiny new independence the board had enjoyed since 1970 was soon removed, though environmental studies continued to ensure that the anticipated demands of government in this area would be met.

The joint effort of Trunk Line and TransCanada to get the Arctic Gas group to examine seriously the pros and cons of a pipeline using existing pipeline systems wherever possible and a whole new pipeline from the Arctic across Canada to the U.S. boundary never seems to have had any success. Trunk Line complained in a ten-page memo in January 1973 that the Arctic Gas management, instead of comparing the two approaches, had produced a statement that amounted to ''an indictment'' of the idea of expanding existing Canadian systems, and support of the single-line approach.

The Arctic Gas management began developing a policy for financing the pipeline in earnest in May 1973. The policy soon became an extensive amplification of the policy line taken from the beginning by the Northwest Group, and the emphasis was further away than ever from the Environmental Protection Board's. The previously mentioned Craik-Calef paper had already stated that one of the Arctic gas pipeline challenges was to incorporate the environmental costs into a cost-benefit analysis. The Arctic Gas management policy disagreed with that viewpoint; it advocated instead, one source informed me, that the routing of the pipeline should be determined primarily by the economics of the project.

The Arctic Gas management policy also took the position that financing implications arose primarily as a consequence of ownership — not routing. The belief was expressed in top-level discussions that to assure the highest probability of success in financing the pipeline, it should be a coordinated construction project — a unified undertaking. The general thrust of the policy was that the bigger the companies participating, the easier the pipeline financing. One of the most important elements in raising so much money would be an unlimited completion undertaking by all parties participating.

A policy report for management pointed out that lenders would regard the pipeline as a single integrated project. They would also require that a financially responsible group be able to coordinate and influence the policies of the project for the benefit of the undertaking as a whole.

The Merger Unmerges
The infighting for control of Canadian Arctic Gas Study Group Limited/Canadian Arctic Gas Pipeline Limited continued over a wide field during 1973 and 1974, with the forces headed by Robert Blair gradually losing one fight after another to the majority on the management of the merged group.

The design of the corporate vehicle through which the financing would be done was settled in an Arctic Gas management memo dated 15 May 1973. It incorporated the earlier recommendations and rejected the TransCanada-Trunk Line approach. A nine-page memo said that the financing for the entire project must be arranged as a single unified undertaking. It could not be financed piecemeal, over time. Rather, all funds to finance the entire project must be raised or committed at the outset, before drawdown of any portion. Project financing will require that there be equality of underlying security covenants for all segments of the project.

The Arctic Gas management had also accepted a policy viewpoint against multiple ownership of the line for another reason. According to this viewpoint, Trunk Line and TransCanada have not of themselves sufficient financial strength to provide the necessary equality of underlying security covenants (guarantees) to those required for other segments of the projects. Consequently, a situation was foreseen where, under multiple ownership, guarantors of other sections of the line would have to back the Trunk Line and TransCanada sections as well. "We see no compelling economic reason for such other guarantors to extend such covenants to arms-length companies," the memo concluded.

The Arctic Gas management decided that multiple ownership of the pipeline would have "serious adverse consequences on the form and feasibility of the project's ultimate financing," and accordingly recommended that the entire Canadian project "be constructed and owned by" Canadian Arctic Gas Pipeline.

By the time that Arctic Gas filed its formal application with the National Energy Board on 21 March 1974, the question of whether or not to seek government financial help for the pipeline had been hotly debated for months behind the scenes within the management committee. At a meeting in Los Angeles on 10 January 1974, chairman W. P. Wilder opened a discussion on financing, by stating that he hoped the financing could be arranged without government help. A 17 February 1974 memo from E. W. Unruh, a Standard Oil vice-president, said, however: "Sohio believes that the present project financing plan is not feasible and that the project can only be accomplished if adequate financial support from the governments of both the United States and Canada is obtained."

The Sohio position was accepted eventually, but when the CAGPL application was initially filed, it included the provision that financial plans and Canadian content would be provided "subsequent to the date of this application."

Alberta Gas Trunk Line went along with the initial Arctic Gas application, but with strong reservations. As various newspapers noted at the time, the Arctic Gas application ran to 7,000 pages of detail on engineering, environmental impact, the pipeline's route and possible alternatives to it; however, still missing was any information about the project's viability in terms of financing, costs, tariffs, supplies and marketing, and the impact of such a massive undertaking on the Canadian economy. In statements to the news media at the time, both Vernon Horte and Wilder made it very clear that, without access to Alaskan gas, their proposed pipeline would not be economic as a carrier of Canadian gas from the Mackenzie Delta alone.

In February 1974, Robert Blair wrote a letter to the Premier of Alberta to inform him about his growing uneasiness with the merger. "In Alberta Gas Trunk Line we do not have confidence that the present internationally-controlled project proposal of Canadian Arctic Gas Study Limited will be able to succeed or that it is the right proposal at all." (By then Alberta had a new premier, Peter Lougheed, whose Progressive Conservative party forces had defeated the Social Credit Government headed by Harry Strom in August 1971.) Blair's letter went on to say that:

> The present CAGPL proposal is still founded mainly on the movement of Alaskan gas to United States markets and on allegedly small available quantities of Mackenzie Delta gas to United States markets also, with only peripheral consideration of future gas supply to Canadian markets and with little in it for local interests across western Canada. We think it is far too much oriented to United States markets and we also know it is facing really heavy internal difficulties in obtaining financing commitments.

Blair also reminded the Premier about Trunk Line's earlier reservations about merging with the Northwest Group.

Then, on 22 May 1974, Blair delivered a statement to an Arctic Gas management committee meeting in which he informed other members that Alberta Gas Trunk Line had been looking into an alternative to the Arctic Gas project for which an application had been filed two months earlier. Trunk Line had become convinced that if obstacles to the Arctic Gas project proved too great — among them Blair mentioned financing and availability of enough 48-inch pipe — a 42-inch diameter pipeline from Canada's Beaufort basin south would be an economic alternative.

Rumours that Trunk Line was planning to pull out of Arctic Gas appeared in the news media in late July 1974. In reaction, Blair issued a six-page public statement at the end of an Arctic Gas management committee meeting in Toronto on July 31, after discussing the statement with others on the committee. It said that Trunk Line was continuing as a member of the study group, but had developed "a contingency plan" to connect Canadian Arctic gas to Canadian markets. The plan for a smaller pipeline, at an estimated cost then of $1.75 billion, was outlined, as was the rationale behind it. The statement estimated that it could be completed within two and a half years of approval; it also emphasized that this plan was not intended at all to exclude transmission of Alaska gas across Canada.

Some of the unpublicized reasons behind Blair's move had been explained in an April 18 letter to the Alberta Minister of Mines and Minerals, then W. D. (Bill) Dickie:

> In our company, we are distressed with the trend of events connected with the filing of the Arctic gas pipeline application by Canadian Arctic Gas Pipeline Limited. Our distress is in two directions. First, we do not believe that the application as filed, by majority vote of the twenty-seven members, is sufficiently tailored to meet the future commercial involvement of our own company or of gas services in and for the province as reflected through our operations. Second, we judge that the project applied for may not be a practical proposal when assessed in the whole range of considerations covering ownership, financing, service to Canadian markets and political acceptability in Canada.

For these reasons, Blair said, Trunk Line had found "our own enthusiasm turning toward an alternative plan.''

When Robert Blair began, during the summer of 1974, to think about withdrawing Trunk Line from the Arctic Gas group, as far as he knew at that time, his company would then have to face alone all the other companies in the huge international consortium. Then word leaked out, and he confirmed that Trunk Line was working on the Maple Leaf line idea, though still a member of the Arctic Gas group for the time being. Very shortly afterward, Blair received a telephone call from the then chairman and chief executive officer of Westcoast Transmission Company Limited, Kelly H. Gibson. He asked to see Blair in his Trunk Line office on the following Saturday morning. To Blair's surprise, Gibson expressed his interest in making Westcoast Transmission a partner in the Maple Leaf project. But first, Gibson said, Trunk Line should withdraw from the Arctic Gas group.

By then, Gibson said in an interview, Westcoast had turned down several invitations to join the Arctic Gas group. It had seemed to Gibson that the Arctic Gas group, with as many as 28 companies among its membership at one point, was "always fussing" and had a lot of trouble making decisions. He was by then convinced that any Arctic gas pipeline across Canada should be, and could be, built by the three major Canadian pipeline companies: Westcoast Transmission, Alberta Gas Trunk Line and TransCanada PipeLines. But TransCanada had taken up wholeheartedly with the Arctic Gas group. "So I went to Bob and said, 'Why don't you pull out and then we'll join you and support you?'" Gibson recalled.

A hard-nosed veteran of the Canadian oil scene, Kelly H. Gibson enjoys a wide reputation as an outstanding free enterprise entrepreneur. Born in Broken Arrow, Oklahoma, on 19 March 1912, Gibson arrived in Alberta in 1949 as a Gulf Oil specialist in petroleum well drilling and production. He never left and his reputation grew steadily, until in 1957 he was invited to join the fledgling Pacific Petroleums Limited, headed by Frank McMahon of the Calgary-launched family famous throughout the oil patch for its flamboyance and swift rise to wealth on petroleum earnings. During his 17 years with Pacific Pete, Gibson rose quickly from vice-president to the position of president and chief executive officer in May 1964. He also became chairman and chief executive officer of Westcoast Transmission in July 1970. He retired from Pacific Petroleums in 1974 and as chairman of the Westcoast board in March 1977. He stayed on, however, as chairman and director of Foothills Pipe Lines Limited, the subsidiary which Westcoast bought into from Trunk Line, following Gibson's Saturday morning meeting with Blair.

From the success which his leadership had given to both Pacific Petroleums and Westcoast Transmission, Gibson brought to the Maple Leaf project, and later to the Alaska Highway project, a capitalist respectability that Blair lacked because of Trunk Line's creation by the Alberta government. Trunk Line still remains a strange object treated with wariness by much of the oil industry in Canada for this reason. Although he has been a Canadian citizen since August 1964, Gibson's American birth and background helped to off-balance Blair's reputation as an Albertan and Canadian nationalist.

At their Saturday morning meeting, Blair learned that Gibson had been watching Blair's manoeuvring to keep control of any Arctic gas pipeline in Canadian hands for some time, and that Gibson approved of this goal and wanted to help Blair achieve it. Blair remembered that meeting with some emotion. At that point, for all his outward confidence in the Maple Leaf proposal, Blair badly needed such a voluntary and uninvited vote of confidence. It was particularly welcome coming from such a noted entrepreneur as Kelly Gibson. They closed the deal with a handshake.

Blair thought about it for a little longer, then decided that the new plan would be more than Trunk Line could support while still remaining a member of the Arctic Gas group. He was also encouraged to withdraw by his new partner, whose visit chance had timed almost perfectly.

On 13 September 1974 Trunk Line officially notified all participants in the Arctic Gas group of its withdrawal, which it then announced publicly three days later.

Without doubt, the boldest gamble of several he has risked in 26 years as a pipeliner was Blair's decision in 1974 to pull out of the union between his and Horte's groups, and to propose a new project of his own (from here on, for the sake of simplicity, Blair's new group will be referred to as Foothills) for piping Arctic gas to southern markets. In the opinion of Horte and like-minded critics of Blair, his gamble was totally unnecessary, if not foolhardy, and perhaps vainglorious as well. Horte told me that he was convinced Blair had never wanted to join up with his group — though Blair denied this. Horte also said that Blair was welcome back in his group if he wanted to rejoin. "I personally never expected him to stay in," Horte said. "His main objection in my opinion was that he always wanted absolutely to own any gas pipeline that went through Alberta." Horte would undoubtedly also agree that Blair's attitude throughout supports the judgment made of him in February 1977 by Toronto *Star* Ottawa columnist Richard Gwyn. Following a few days' visit to Alberta, which included an interview with Blair, Gwyn described him as "a fanatic Alberta nationalist."

However Blair's 1974 decision might be viewed, the oil industry can have witnessed few larger acts of defiance against its most powerful barons. Blair's decision to withdraw from the Arctic Gas consortium left Alberta Gas Trunk Line playing a lone hand again (except for Westcoast Transmission), since all of his American former partners stayed behind, adding their substantial strength to the already formidable forces of Arctic Gas. Moreover, among the Arctic Gas forces were not only major owners and producers of gas (gas which the newly-hatched project that Blair proposed would transmit if it ever got into the permafrost), but most of the potential customers for this gas in Canada as well as in the United States.

The most powerful opponent of all was Exxon Corporation, which was still — though perhaps slightly shaken by OPEC's 1973 takeover of world oil price control — managing the globe's oldest and biggest multinational oil empire from offices high over Manhattan and Houston. And not only the biggest *oil* multinational, but the biggest multinational *period*. (Just to give you some idea: Exxon reported in January 1977 that its profits in 1976 totaled $2.64 billion. That was $14 million more than the Northwest Group, of which Exxon was a leading member, originally estimated in 1970 that the Arctic gas pipeline would cost. Exxon's total 1976 revenue rose to $52.68 billion from $48.7 billion in 1975. In his budget speech on 25 May 1976, Finance Minister Donald Macdonald estimated that Canadian government spending for the fiscal year 1976-77 would be about $42.1 billion; revenues would be about $37.7 billion for a deficit of $4.4 billion. That is how awesome an opponent Exxon can be.) Exxon's subsidiary, Humble Oil, has already been discussed. Another member of Arctic Gas was Exxon's Canadian subsidiary, Imperial Oil Limited of Toronto, a major holder of new gas reserves in Canada's western Arctic region.

Also represented in the consortium, as it still is, was the world's second-largest oil multinational, the Shell Group with headquarters in London and The Hague, reflecting its joint British-Dutch ownership. Gulf, yet another of the top oil multinationals, was represented by one of its subsidiaries, Gulf Oil Canada Limited of Toronto.

By 1974 just those three of the Seven Sisters were major, if not dominant, owners of the known gas reserves both on Alaska's North Slope and in Canada's western Arctic. No gas pipeline south from the Arctic could do business without doing business with them.

Blair's action was also open defiance of Trunk Line's biggest Canadian customer — TransCanada PipeLines Limited, whose former president and director, Vernon L. Horte, had since September 1972 been president of the Arctic Gas Group. Although TransCanada listed its head office as Calgary, its executive offices are in Toronto's Commerce Court East. The traditional eastern Canadian business assumption of superiority over western Canadian business, a tradition especially associated with Toronto, had now openly inserted itself as another issue in the Arctic gas pipeline struggle — along with the equally traditional western Canadian resentment of this attitude and dream of future redress.

Blair and his fellow executives at Trunk Line acted, of course, in the knowledge that the final decision about any Arctic gas pipeline lay, not with the private powers in the industry, but initially with the public regulatory agencies of the Canadian and American governments, and finally with those governments themselves. Both the owners of gas in the North and the southern distributors of the gas would have to use whatever pipelines the governments ultimately approved. But Blair's action was still that of a David against a multiplicity of Goliaths.

There was, beyond argument, an element of Alberta provincialism in Blair's decision. There was also an element of Canadian nationalism. But records going back to early 1970 show there was a simple yearning for independence of action, too. The decision seems, from these records, to have been motivated in part at least by Blair's early experience as a Canadian subsidiary boss with an American parent boss always second-guessing over his shoulder.

4

THE CASE OF
MARSHALL CROWE

On 9 July 1975, D. M. M. Goldie, Q.C.. made an unusual call on
Hyman Soloway, special legal counsel of the National Energy
Board in Ottawa. Goldie, a member of the Russell & Du Moulin
firm of barristers and solicitors in Vancouver, made his representation to Soloway on behalf of his client, Canadian Arctic Gas
Pipeline Limited of Toronto. The meeting, requested by Goldie,
set in motion a remarkable process which eventually removed
NEB chairman Marshall Crowe from the centre of the board's
most important assignment ever, the hearing of applications to
build an Arctic gas pipeline.

Goldie's visit raised some eyebrows around the NEB's modest
offices in the Trebla Building west of Parliament Hill at 473 Albert
Street. On the same date, the board completed a two-day pre-
hearing conference to set up procedures for the Arctic gas pipeline
hearing. What Goldie wanted to talk about certainly had to do with
hearing procedure. Acting on instructions from his client, Goldie
had come to suggest that Crowe should disqualify himself from
sitting on any panel assigned to deal with the Arctic Gas and other
applications for the right to build a gas pipeline south from the
Arctic.

So bold and unusual a move was in itself enough to tickle
curiosity. What might have caused mouths to open in surprise as
well was Goldie's timing. At the date of his meeting, the board had
not made public any decision on the makeup of the panel. Did this

constitute an attempt to influence a board decision privately before it became public knowledge?

Goldie's expressions of concern were based on the fact that Crowe, prior to his appointment to the NEB, had been chairman of the Canada Development Corporation — and in that capacity, until his resignation in 1973, had been a CDC representative in the Arctic Gas group. As such, he had participated in certain decisions of the group concerning relevant issues of the application of the group's offspring, Canadian Arctic Gas Pipeline Limited, which would be put before the board. Goldie indicated that it was his intention to seek a ruling to determine the propriety of the makeup of the Arctic pipeline panel, should Crowe be included among its membership.

The exchange was polite, as befits professionals at this sort of thing, but there was an element of terseness and tension in it. Something of this flavour of disciplined propriety can be detected in a letter written on August 19, some five weeks later, to Goldie by Robert A. Stead, the NEB's secretary:

> You presented Board Counsel with selected excerpts from the minutes of the study group which, not unexpectedly, revealed that Mr. Crowe, performing his duties as the representative of Canada Development Corporation, had attended and participated in various meetings of the study group. At no time was there any suggestion that there was, nor did you indicate that you feared, actual bias or proprietary or pecuniary interest insofar as the Chairman was concerned. Your fears were directed to the possibility that, based upon the facts above-stated, any certificate issued to your client might be subject to attack on the grounds that there was reasonable apprehension of bias by the Chairman in favour of your client.

The eight members of the NEB had held several meetings about the Goldie representations. Stead's letter informed him of their decision. They had decided to designate Crowe as chairman of the Arctic pipeline panel. However, "in order to allay any fears or reservations on the part of your client," the letter continued, with a hint of archness in its tone, "as to bias in its favour," Crowe at the opening of the hearing would make a statement. It would cover for all participants and interested parties his previous association with the Canada Development Corporation, and his participation in the Arctic Gas group meetings as the CDC representative.

Crowe had been appointed to the NEB by a government fully cognizant of his background, including his involvement with the Arctic Gas group on behalf of the Canada Development Corporation. The possibility that he could be accused of being in a conflict-of-interest position seemed not to have occurred to anyone but Goldie and his clients. Crowe had no intention of sitting back and letting anyone attack him on those grounds and immediately took the initiative to bring the issue which Goldie raised out into the open before all interested parties.

To ensure that all the material and facts were made available to all interested parties, and by then there were more than 80, the board asked Goldie to deposit at its offices all relevant minutes of Arctic Gas group meetings from the time that CDC had become a member, and correspondence between the group and CDC. Stead also advised Goldie that copies of the letter were being sent to interested parties "so that all parties may be informed as to the concerns which you have expressed."

The day after the letter was written, it was released to the news media, and the Crowe case went public from there on.

What was really behind this Arctic Gas move? Some people with whom I spoke interpreted the outcome of the Crowe case as an awesome example of the lengths to which multinational corporations would go to protect their power. They saw this as proof that a fundamental issue in this pipeline decision was whether Canada would continue to be a branch-plant economy, in which orders from anonymous executives outside Canada could undermine even so powerful a position as the Canadian-government-appointed chairman of the National Energy Board. But who could say with finality whether Goldie was sent on his mission by Arctic Gas on secret orders from Exxon or one of the other large American participants in the study group? Canadian Arctic Gas Pipeline president Vernon Horte was quoted as saying that it was not a matter of his company's lacking faith in Crowe's integrity, but a legal question.

One of the more moderate and informed energy correspondents in Ottawa's Parliamentary Press Gallery, Jeff Carruthers of F.P. Publications (which includes the Toronto *Globe and Mail*), interpreted the content of Stead's letter as revealing a move by Arctic Gas to have Crowe disqualified as a member of any NEB panel hearing the northern pipeline applications. As Carruthers reported in the Calgary *Albertan* on 21 August 1975:

Reliable sources suggest that Canadian Arctic Gas may in fact be more concerned that Mr. Crowe is an avid nationalist and therefore might favor the competing, all-Canadian pipeline being proposed by Foothills Pipe Lines Ltd. of Calgary. Sources also revealed that member companies of the Canadian Arctic Gas group did not seem to be aware of the formal challenge being launched against Marshall Crowe by Canadian Arctic Gas lawyers.

Some of my sources suggested the same thing, though my contacts at Arctic Gas denied any such motives on their part as trying to "get" Crowe, so that his long experience at trying to widen the independence of Canadian enterprise might not stand in the way of their multinational members' ambitions.

Goldie responded to the Stead letter with a brief one of his own on August 28 from his Vancouver office. One paragraph struck Stead as requiring a clarifying reply. This paragraph read: "While I appreciate the Board's agreement with me that this matter is serious and should be dealt with before the hearings commence, I have some concern that the procedure proposed might not achieve its purpose." Goldie said that he would write again after Arctic Gas had a chance to consider his views "in this regard."

In his reply of September 18, Stead referred to the paragraph quoted from Goldie's letter, then made clear that Goldie had presumed more than he perhaps should have:

The letter of the 19th should not be interpreted as an indication of the Board's agreement with your representations at that meeting [with NEB counsel] on any aspects of the hearing, including the seriousness of the matter you raised. The direction sets forth when and how that matter will be dealt with and any party which has concern as to the procedure may make representation at that time.

All correspondence exchanged between Goldie and the board was copied and sent to all other parties interested in the hearings on the Arctic pipeline applications. They were also sent a memo by Stead on October 17, which included with it a copy of the statement that Crowe proposed to make at the opening of the hearing, scheduled for October 27. The memo informed them that each party would afterward be asked to indicate for the record any objection which it might have to Crowe's participation as a member of the panel.

There was an atmosphere of low-keyed tension in the ballroom of Ottawa's Chateau Laurier when the hearing opened at 9 a.m. on Monday 27 October 1975. Ranged in front of the low dais on which Crowe and his fellow panelists, J. A. Farmer and W. A. Scotland, took their places at a long bench-like desk were a total of 79 legal counsel (including 13 Queen's Counsel) and other representatives of interested parties. Altogether, 52 companies and organizations were represented in the ballroom, and a number of others were on the list of intervenors but had not yet appeared.

Marshall Crowe, a tall, slender man whose stern appearance behind his horn-rimmed glasses is softened by a warm smile, was the centre of attention. His gently modulated voice conceals an iron will and a temper which he occasionally unleashes to clear the minds of recalcitrant witnesses. Observers recalled an occasion when Crowe leaned forward across his bench and glared at an oil company witness who did not want to answer a question on the grounds that the information was confidential. "Well, I guess whether you reply depends on how far you want to advance your project," Crowe said, his reddish tinge revealing a flush of anger. He got the information and later told a reporter: "I've got a temper and sometimes it has to show." Then his ready sense of humour showed itself. "Besides," he smiled, "it woke everyone up."

Another figure of interest in the ballroom was, of course, D. M. M. Goldie, a tall bespectacled man with reddish-brown hair, who was heading a team of six lawyers. He spoke that morning for both Canadian and Alaskan Arctic Gas pipelines and for Texas Eastern Transmission, an American member of the Arctic Gas consortium. Another figure worth noting in the ballroom that morning was John B. Ballem of Calgary, like Goldie a Queen's Counsel. A man of quiet self-possession, Ballem was representing three of the Seven Sisters — Exxon through Imperial Oil Limited, Gulf through Gulf Oil Canada Limited, and Shell through Shell Canada Limited. Three others present were less prominent, but were to play key roles in the drama to follow: A. R. Lucas of the Canadian Arctic Resources Committee, John A. Olthuis of the Committee for Justice and Liberty Foundation, and Andrew J. Roman of the Consumers' Association of Canada.

The board had made an exception to its usual rules about news media coverage of its deliberations. Usually, television cameras and radio microphones were barred, but both were allowed that morning to record the opening statement of the chairman. Crowe opened the proceedings with a cheery "Good morning, ladies and gentlemen," as though he could not really believe that anyone would seriously accuse him of being capable of exercising bias in a decision.

After a few more introductory lines, Crowe said: "The hearing itself is unprecedented in terms of its magnitude and the pervasiveness of its issues." No one would dispute that. For the first time, he went on, the board was hearing applications to move gas from frontier areas. "The filings reflect a wider scope of inquiry than any the board has undertaken," he said. (The National Energy Board was established in 1959.) This wide spectrum of interest was represented in the various intervenors ready to participate. In the course of making a decision on the Arctic pipeline applications, many related findings would have to be made, "each of which will affect Canada's energy future."

Then Crowe turned the proceedings over to Hyman Soloway, who had to deal with some routine business, including the rather tedious chore of identifying all interested parties present and their representatives. The reporters leaned back and paid little attention while this was going on, then grew attentive again as Crowe prepared to deliver the statement which he had already circulated. After a few preliminary remarks, he briefly summarized his career up to the present critical moment.

In November 1971, he had left a position in the Public Service of Canada which he had held for some four years, a position as deputy secretary to the federal cabinet with responsibility for operations, which had kept him in intimate contact with the centre of political power in Canada. (It was during the early period of this part of Crowe's career that I had met him. From the start, he struck me as one of Canada's rarer bureaucrats, for his competence, detached objectivity toward the uses of power, and rueful good humour about the privileges and problems of government employment. As far as Crowe's integrity as a public servant is concerned, I concede unconditionally my prejudice in his favour.) He left this position to take an appointment by Prime Minister Pierre Trudeau, through a cabinet order-in-council, as a provisional director of the newly established Canada Development Corporation. He was subsequently elected a director and later became president of the CDC.

A year after Crowe joined the CDC, it became, on 30 November 1972, an official member of the Gas Arctic Northwest Project Study Group, the consortium which established Canadian Arctic

Gas Pipeline Limited. Pending formal membership, however, Crowe attended his first meeting of Arctic Gas on 25 October 1972, a session of its executive committee. Crowe was there, and at two other executive committee meetings, as an observer. The group's membership ranged from 26 to 28 companies while Crowe was a participant. For voting purposes, the group's membership was divided into three categories of roughly nine participants each: Canadian non-producers, United States non-producers, and producers. Crowe was a member of the group's management committee, which was composed of one representative from each of the participating companies. A decision of the management committee required a favourable vote of the majority of members of each of the three participant groups. The management committee delegated some of its functions to an executive committee, which consisted of three representatives from each of the three participant groups.

During his two years at the CDC, Crowe had attended seven monthly meetings of the management committee and three meetings of the executive committee. At a management committee meeting on 26 September 1972, he moved the resolution appointing the group's project banking advisers. He was also on a steering committee which recommended the project financial advisers and accounting advisers. These advisers included Wood Gundy, the firm from which the group's chairman, W. P. Wilder, had been recruited.

There was a story to be heard in the rarer reaches of the Canadian oil patch which perhaps revealed as much about the Crowe case as any other, though I was unable to confirm it with any of the principals. It may be apocryphal, for all I could tell, but I did not doubt that it was true to Crowe's character and courage and belief in independence for Canadian business enterprise.

As this story goes, Crowe arrived one evening at the Royal York Hotel in Toronto for a meeting there the following morning. In the lobby he encountered an Exxon representative, who invited Crowe to join him and a few other American members of the study group for a nightcap in the bar. It was an informal group and no one bothered about introductions. The talk got around to the choice of financial advisers, and one American executive let it be known he did not think much of the Canadian choice that was to be offered them the next day, namely Wood Gundy. His preference was for Morgan Stanley, the New York firm that served as financial advisers to Exxon, but he guessed they had better give the Canadians their way about Wood Gundy. Displaying a southern U.S. sense of humour, the man chuckled and supposedly said something along the line of: "As long as we know Morgan Stanley is really running things, I guess it's okay to have our good Canadian nigger in the backdoor."

Not everyone laughed. In fact, hardly anyone did, and there was even a moment or two of silence, maybe uneasy silence. Then, so this story went, Marshall Crowe politely introduced himself to the man and told him which firm he represented. Others around the table joined the American executive in trying to dismiss his remarks as just barfly banter, but Crowe was not the type to let the American off his hook so easily. He told his Exxon friend that he thought the man should be sent back to the U.S. on the next plane. There was no way that Crowe would ever do business with such a person again. Next morning, so my story ended, the American executive did not appear at the management committee meeting, nor at any others that Crowe attended.

Between 7 December 1972 and 27 June 1973, Crowe continued in his statement at the hearing on opening day, the study group had considered a number of possible routes for the portion of the pipeline south of the 60th parallel. One issue was whether it should be an all-new pipeline or consist of an expansion of the facilities of Alberta Gas Trunk Line. After extensive review and discussion, the final decision had been that facilities in Alberta would be owned by Arctic Gas and that the route would parallel the existing Trunk Line system, but on a separate right-of-way.

In the spring of 1973 Crowe became chairman of the board of the CDC, but effective on October 15 of the same year, he resigned to accept the chairmanship of the National Energy Board, another order-in-council appointment in which the Prime Minister normally had a final say. On his NEB appointment, Crowe had also resigned from the study group management committee. He explained:

From the 30th of October, 1972, to the date of my resignation from the CDC . . . my participation in the study group was at all times as a representative of this government-owned organization and was but one of my responsibilities as president and chairman of the CDC. Canadian Arctic Gas Pipeline Limited, through Mr. Goldie, its counsel, expressed concern that my previous association with the study group might give rise to a reasonable apprehension of bias in its favor. At no time was there any suggestion, nor did Mr. Goldie indicate that he or his client feared, that I had, or have had, actual bias or proprietary or pecuniary interest.

Crowe pointed out that all interested parties now had full access to relevant correspondence and other facts about this issue. "It need hardly be stated," said Crowe, "that my fellow members of the panel and I propose to assume and to discharge our duties and exercise our powers on the evidence and in the public interest." However, if any person had "a reasonable apprehension of bias on my part," he concluded, "that person has a right to object."

Soloway then proposed a brief adjournment, to which Crowe agreed, and after the break, Soloway asked Ian A. Blue of his staff to call out the name of each interested party and to have it state on the record whether it had any objection so far as the chairman's position was concerned.

Was what happened next really the way it appeared? Or was it, as some suspect, one of the more clever Machiavellian manoeuvres of modern Canadian times? Had it been the intention of Arctic Gas executives simply to raise the issue, then sit back with hands piously folded and defend Crowe's honour, while more romantic interests at the hearing picked up this fine moral issue and ran with it from there, they could scarcely have wished for greater success. Still, for anyone with such a plan in mind, there remained a few minutes more of tension before the issue was finally joined.

The first name which Blue called out was that of Arctic Gas. Had it any objection to Crowe sitting on the panel? Goldie responded: "No." Three times more, Goldie gave the same response, for Alaskan Arctic Gas, Northern Border Pipeline, and Texas Eastern Transmission.

The first to respond for the Foothills group was the vice-president of Foothills Pipe Lines, Calgary lawyer R. J. (Reg) Gibbs, Q.C. A man of average height with dark hair and mustache, a morose expression habitually on his face, but alert eyes ever-watchful behind his spectacles, Gibbs rose and joined the chorus of "nos."

When his turn came, Ballem gave Crowe the vocal support of Dome Petroleum Limited, along with that of Gulf, Shell and Imperial.

Blue had drawn 55 "nos" and 8 "no-shows" by the time he called out the sixty-fourth name, that of the Canadian Arctic Resources Committee (CARC). Its representative, A. R. Lucas, rose. "Mr. Chairman," he said, "I have been instructed to formally object."

On what basis, Blue asked.

"The basis of the objection is the association of Mr. Crowe with CDC and in his capacity as an officer of that corporation," Lucas replied, "and the participation in meetings of the Arctic Gas study group, as indicated in the material filed by Arctic Gas."

Blue asked when CARC had first become aware of this past association. Lucas replied there was an awareness prior to the Arctic Gas disclosures, "but the details of that association were not known until the material filed by Arctic Gas was revealed."

Were there any other grounds, Blue asked.

Lucas replied that there was one more, based on articles in the Toronto *Star* drawn from an as-yet unpublished book, *The National Interest* by York University professor Edmond Dosman. It told of a meeting on 12 May 1970 of a number of senior federal public servants, including Crowe in his capacity as a deputy Cabinet secretary, at which "the essential content" of the federal government's 1970 northern pipeline guidelines had been drawn up.

"Professor Dosman suggests that those guidelines amount to approval in principle for a Mackenzie Valley gas pipeline," Lucas said. That being so, Crowe would have been involved in consideration of technical, financial, economic and environmental viability of the Mackenzie Valley gas pipeline, Lucas went on, "the very issues that are to be determined in relation to the applications now before the board."

"Our submission," Lucas said, "is that these matters raised in the book might well suggest to a reasonable person a likelihood, or at least raise an apprehension, of bias."

Soloway asked Lucas if he would provide him with more details about the articles, and Blue resumed calling out the names. A spokesman for the Canadian Wildlife Federation said it had no objection to Crowe. Nor had the Committee for an Independent Canada. Then Olthuis objected on behalf of the Committee on Justice and Liberty Foundation, but not out of any reasonable apprehension that Crowe might favour Arctic Gas. His group's apprehension was that Crowe might be biased in favour of the need for a pipeline at all — which his group considered "the critical issue in these hearings."

Olthuis said that his group assumed Crowe was determined to adjudicate the applications in good faith, but doubted his past involvements with the pipeline issues could help but affect his impartiality. "Accordingly," he concluded, "we submit that it is in the interest of public justice that Mr. Crowe remove himself from this panel."

A few moments later, Andrew Roman, speaking on behalf of the Consumers' Association of Canada, ensured that Crowe's case would not be settled that day. The CAC took no position on whether Crowe might be biased toward one of the applications. However, any member of a regulatory tribunal "must be guided by the principle that he ought not to sit on any matter where there exists a reasonable apprehension of bias," Roman said. But determining whether such a reasonable apprehension existed was something that required an objective, not a subjective, test. Since the CAC could only make a subjective analysis, it could neither object to Crowe's presence on the panel nor not object. It could only comment, and his suggestion was that the issue be referred to the Federal Court of Appeal for adjudication.

Although no one else raised objections to Crowe's being on the panel, the board adjourned as soon as the last group had been heard from.

Reporting the opening day of the hearing in the Ottawa *Journal* the next afternoon, Jeff Carruthers wrote that some observers had described it as "the crucifixion of Marshall Crowe." The Canadian Arctic Resources Committee, an environmental group, and the Committee on Justice and Liberty Foundation, a nondenominational religious group, had "stepped into the trap and set out to accomplish what Canadian Arctic Gas wanted all along." Carruthers added, "the removal of Mr. Crowe from the panel because he is suspected to have nationalistic leanings which might go against the joint Canada-U.S. project." Without elaborating, Carruthers noted that Arctic Gas had raised the Crowe bias issue "in what was considered a less than forthright manner."

Two days later, on 29 October 1975, Crowe submitted the issue to the Federal Court of Appeals. He and others at the NEB had come to the conclusion there was no alternative after two days of private considerations.

Writing in the Toronto *Globe and Mail* of 4 November 1975,

business columnist Ronald Anderson interpreted this result as success by Arctic Gas "in its efforts to obtain a legal decision" on Crowe's role. The actions of Arctic Gas, he wrote, "create a suspicion" that it would rest more easily if Crowe were removed from the panel. "The NEB chairman's career has been largely that of a career civil servant whose primary concern has been to protect the interests of the Canadian public," Anderson noted. Though Arctic Gas, after raising the issue, had offered no objection to Crowe itself, it had "in effect tossed the ball to the public interest, or sectional groups who were looking for an issue."

The case went to the Federal Court in December 1975. During the three days of argument (December 8, 9 and 10) the public interest groups, which now included the CAC, made no attempt to suggest that Crowe was actually biased. They concentrated on proving the existence of a "reasonable apprehension of bias." Toronto lawyer Ian Binnie argued on behalf of the Committee for Justice and Liberty: "Mr. Crowe's motives are not on trial. What is on trial is whether the people who will be affected by the decision of the NEB on the Mackenzie Valley pipeline might have a reasonable apprehension that the decision was arrived at without any bias."

Soloway and other lawyers supporting Crowe (including Michael Goldie), argued that the decisions made by Arctic Gas while Crowe was a member of the management committee were "extremely vague" and that the group was only carrying on "exploratory" studies. Its application had not been filed with the NEB until the spring of 1974, some five months after Crowe had left the group. However, Binnie made the point that Crowe had been present, as his own statement showed, at the meeting where the routing and ownership of the proposed pipeline had been unanimously decided. Now, Binnie said, "Mr. Crowe is going to have to review a plan of which he himself is an architect. One cannot get away from this fact and, therefore, Mr. Crowe should be disqualified from this hearing. It is only by doing so that the public will have confidence the NEB had a fresh, second look at the pipeline scheme."

The Federal Court of Appeals handed down its judgment on 12 December 1975. The question which Crowe had submitted was brief: "Would the board err in rejecting the objections and in holding that Mr. Crowe was not disqualified from being a member of the panel on the grounds of reasonable apprehension or reasonable likelihood of bias?''

The court's unanimous five-member decision was even briefer: "No."

The reasons for judgment first dealt with the claim by Lucas on behalf of CARC that Crowe had participated in a meeting of federal bureaucrats in May 1970 that had been critical in writing the federal guidelines issued that August for Northern pipelines. The court noted that Crowe had informed it, in a statement, that this meeting was "not directed to nor was it critical in hammering out the essential content of the 1970 guidelines." Since nothing was presented to substantiate this claim by Lucas, the court regarded that objection as withdrawn.

The reasons for judgment then referred to "the very painstaking and thorough arguments put before us by counsel" — 19 altogether. The variety of opinions drawn from past legal cases, going back as far as 1881 and from countries as distant as Australia and New Zealand, might be due, said the court, "to the fact that bias can be established in a variety of ways." But even in cases where there had been some promise made to an applicant, or a financial interest, or failure to disclose some other interest, "it becomes necessary to consider whether there is reason to apprehend that the person whose duty it is to decide will not listen to the evidence and decide fairly." The court's judgment continued:

Here, neither actual bias nor financial interest are alleged and there is no suggestion in the evidence of any public or private statement by Mr. Crowe or of any promise by him to anyone that any particular result will attend any of the applications. It is true that all of the circumstances of the case, including the decisions in which Mr. Crowe participated as a member of the study group, might give rise in a very sensitive or scrupulous conscience to the uneasy suspicion that he might be unconsciously biased, and therefore should not serve. But that is not, we think, the test to apply in this case. It is, rather, what would an informed person, viewing the matter realistically and practically — and having thought the matter through — conclude? Would he think that it is more likely than not that Mr. Crowe, whether consciously or unconsciously, would not decide fairly?

. . . we are all of the opinion that they should not cause reasonable and right-minded persons to have a reasonable apprehension of bias on the part of Mr. Crowe, either on the question of whether present or future public convenience and necessity require a pipeline or the question of which, if any, of the several applicants should be granted a certificate.

Crowe had participated in the study group not in his own interest, but in the Canadian government's. At no stage did he stand to lose or to gain by this participation. Nor had he anything to lose or gain by any decision he reached as chairman of the NEB, whether in accord with or different from decisions which he had supported in the study group. There appeared to be no reason for apprehension that Crowe would be unable or unwilling to disabuse his mind of preconceptions if new material pointed to a different view, or that he would be unconsciously influenced by decisions he supported as a member of the study group.

Two years had passed since Crowe left the Arctic Gas group. The issues to be resolved by the NEB were "widely different" from those the study group had before it during Crowe's time on it. The issue the NEB had to consider was whether the Canadian public interest would be served by construction and operation of the pipeline and if so, which, if any, among competing applicants should be approved. Crowe was not fettered by any interest of his own in any of the applicant companies. He had no proprietary interest in the result of any decision in which he participated in the study group.

"There appears to be no valid reason," the court decision, written by Mr. Justice A. L. Thurlow, concluded, "for apprehension that Mr. Crowe . . . cannot approach these new issues with the equanimity and impartiality to be expected of one in his position."

In announcing the NEB's decision to send his case to the Federal Court of Appeal, Crowe had also said that the pipeline hearing would continue until a decision was given. Following the December ruling clearing Crowe, the hearing went rapidly ahead.

The three public interest groups, however, were not finished. On 16 January 1976, they served notice on the NEB and other interested parties that they planned to ask the Supreme Court of Canada for leave to appeal the Federal Court of Appeal decision.

The application for leave to appeal was heard by three of the

Supreme Court's nine justices — Chief Justice Bora Laskin and Justices Judson and Spence. The young Toronto lawyer, Ian Binnie, again represented the three public interest groups. He reviewed much the same argument that he had made before the Federal Court and concluded by emphasizing again that there was no suggestion that Crowe had any direct or personal pecuniary interest in the pipeline applications. But if the NEB did approve the Arctic Gas application, Crowe's earlier judgment to spend Canada Development Corporation funds on the study group would be vindicated. (Information given to the Federal Court of Appeal had included the fact that CDC had terminated its active membership in the Arctic Gas study group as of 31 October 1975.)

When G. W. Ainslie, counsel for the Attorney-General of Canada, rose to begin his argument, Chief Justice Laskin asked what possible interest the Attorney-General of Canada could have in this case. Ainslie replied that the Attorney-General had been a party to the case before the Federal Court, and it was even more important to be represented before the Supreme Court. He went on to argue that the Federal Court had made no error in law that would warrant the Supreme Court hearing an appeal. Its decision had applied the proper legal test — whether a reasonable man would have a reasonable apprehension of bias.

The Chief Justice interrupted again, this time with a proposition. It proved to be prophetic. Laskin's proposition went something like this: A lawyer advises a client he has a cause for legal action. The client instructs the lawyer to proceed and the lawyer does. But just before the action comes to trial, the lawyer is appointed a judge. Could the lawyer, in his new role as judge, hear the case he himself had launched? Ainslie replied that under those circumstances, the answer would have to be "no."

When Ian Blue rose to present the NEB's case, Laskin commented that he was "uneasy" about the fact that a board, whose actions were being challenged in a court hearing, was appearing and arguing on its behalf. Blue replied that he felt it was proper for boards to appear before the courts to argue questions of their jurisdiction.

While Goldie was supporting the case against leave to appeal, Mr. Justice Spence asked him a question similar to the one Laskin had asked Ainslie. Again the reply was that a lawyer appointed to the bench could not hear a case as judge that he had prepared as a lawyer.

At the conclusion of argument, the three justices conferred briefly among themselves. Then Laskin announced that leave to appeal was granted.

Because of the urgent need for a decision, so that the pipeline hearing would not be unduly delayed, the appeal was heard beginning March 8. Eight of the nine justices were on the bench when the hearing began. They saved their stiffest questioning for Ainslie, as he put the case for the Attorney-General of Canada on behalf of the federal government. His central argument was that, because Parliament had given the NEB discretionary powers and information-seeking responsibilities, the doctrine of apprehension of bias should be applied differently to NEB members than to members of other judicial or quasi-judicial bodies such as courts. The NEB had a mandate not to make decisions based only on the evidence presented before it during a formal hearing. The basis for making the same decision changed at different times. What was important in this case was what Crowe thought about Northern pipelines now, not what he might have thought two years or more ago.

Chief Justice Laskin asked whether this meant the NEB was exempt from the legal test of apprehension of bias. The test, Ainslie replied, had to be adapted to "the nature and function being undertaken" by the NEB. Mr. Justice R. A. Ritchie said that this argument "doesn't mean a thing to me." Later, Laskin said that Ainslie's argument could only be interpreted as meaning the NEB was exempt from operating without apprehension of bias.

Ainslie argued that the decision to build a Northern pipeline had been taken by the study group before Crowe had joined it. Laskin countered that by joining the study group, the CDC and Crowe had committed themselves to what the group was doing. Ainslie replied that a reasonable person would not find any apprehension of bias.

Laskin responded: "I'm a reasonable person and I'm a little bit concerned about the whole operation."

On the second day of the hearing, it was abruptly adjourned at 3 p.m. until the following morning because Mr. Justice Ritchie suddenly became ill. He was not present the following day, when much of the argument on Crowe's behalf was made and the hearing was concluded. However, the following day, March 11, he joined the Chief Justice and three other justices in the majority judgment issued against Crowe. The argument he had missed had been taped for him to hear later.

Had one more of the justices dissented with Laskin's judgment, the court would have produced a tied verdict — in which case the appeal against Crowe's hearing the Arctic pipeline applications would automatically have failed.

In the reasons for judgment issued later, Laskin wrote the explanation for the majority ruling. In his opinion, "the only issue here is whether the principle of reasonable apprehension or reasonable likelihood of bias applies to the board" for a hearing like that into the Northern pipeline. All involved in the case had agreed that this principle did apply. That being so, wrote Laskin, "I can see no answer" to the position of the three appealing public interest groups. The Chief Justice continued:

> We are not dealing with a case where Mr. Crowe's association with the study group is, by virtue of that fact alone, urged as a disqualification. . . . While I would not see any vice in Mr. Crowe sitting on an application coming from or through the study group in relation to a matter in which he was not involved, even though it was decided upon shortly after his dissociation from the study group, that is not this case.

At another point, Laskin wrote that "the vice of reasonable apprehension of bias lies not in finding correspondence between the decisions in which Mr. Crowe participated" in the study group and the decision that the board must make. It lay, rather, "in the fact that he participated in working out some, at least, of the terms on which the application was later made and supported the decision to make it."

The Federal Court of Appeal had "introduced considerations into its test of reasonable apprehension of bias which should not be part of its measure." The concern here was that there be "no prejudgment of issues (and certainly no predetermination) relating not only to whether a particular application for a pipeline will succeed, but also to whether any pipeline will be approved. . . ." Crowe's participation in discussions and decisions leading to the Arctic Gas application ". . . cannot but give rise to a reasonable apprehension, which reasonably well-informed persons could properly have, of a biased appraisal and judgment of the issues to be determined. . . ."

The test of reasonable apprehension of bias was "grounded in a firm concern that there be no lack of public confidence in the impartiality of the adjudicative agencies." The emphasis was lent to this concern in the Crowe case "by the fact the National Energy Board is enjoined to have regard for the public interest."

The explanation of the dissenting view was written by Mr. Justice de Grandpré. He and his fellow-dissenters, Justices Martland and Judson, found that the Federal Court of Appeal had correctly expressed the proper test to be applied in a matter of this type. The grounds for a reasonable apprehension of bias must be "substantial" and held by "reasonable and right-minded persons." The dissenting judgment entirely agreed with the Federal Court's refusal to accept that the test be related to the "very sensitive or scrupulous conscience." Grandpré went on to say that:

> This is the proper approach which, of course, must be adjusted to the facts of the case. The question of bias in a member of a court of justice cannot be examined in the same light as that in a member of an administrative tribunal entrusted by statute with an administrative discretion exercised in the light of its experience and of that of its technical advisers. The basic principle is of course the same, namely that natural justice be rendered. But its application must take into consideration the special circumstances of the tribunal.
>
> Members of administrative boards acquire their expertise by virtue of previous exposure to the industry which they are appointed to regulate. The system would not work if it were not premised on an assertion of faith in those appointed to adjudicate.
>
> The board is not a court nor is it a quasi-judicial body. . . . The decision to be made by the board transcends the interest of the parties and involves the public interest at large. In reaching its decision, the board draws upon its experience, upon the experience of its own experts, upon the experience of all agencies of the Government of Canada and, obviously, is not and cannot be limited to deciding the matter on the sole basis of the representations made before it. It is not possible to apply to such a body the rules of bias governing the conduct of a court of law.

Marshall Crowe was in Calgary when the final decision was handed down, disqualifying him from continuing to sit on the panel. He announced that he had no intention of resigning from the chairmanship of the board as a result of the judgment (and he remained chairman), but he lost no time in stepping down from the chairmanship of the panel. By mid-March a new panel was named, headed by J. G. Stabback, associate vice-chairman of the board. The two other members were G. G. Edge, also an associate vice-chairman, and R. F. Brooks.

The National Energy Board had adjourned the Northern pipeline hearings in February, after the Supreme Court had agreed to hear the appeal. By then it had spent 34 sitting days hearing evidence on environmental impact and economic efficiency of competing proposals. When the new panel was appointed, it was decided that the hearings would have to start over. The days already passed in sittings were thrown to the winds, along with about a million dollars spent in lawyers' fees, expenses of expert witnesses, and other costs.

In all the public reaction to the Supreme Court's decision, I found none that was critical of Crowe himself. An Ottawa correspondent, Stephen Duncan, writing in the *Financial Post* of 20 March 1976 interpreted the judgment, prematurely it appears, as having "toppled Crowe from the pinnacle of his career." But any criticism to be drawn from the judgment was saved for the federal government. "The court has taken a broad swipe at the Government's style of appointments to quasi-judicial regulatory agencies," Duncan wrote. "If the Government has had this much trouble over Crowe, a distinctly apolitical civil servant, new conflict-of-interest questions could obviously blow up over the appointment of people with strong political connections. . . . What the Supreme Court has done is overturn a Cabinet decision" — its decision to appoint Crowe as still the best man for the job, knowing his background.

The Ottawa *Journal* editorialized that the public interest groups which "pushed" the case to the Supreme Court should not take much satisfaction from the outcome: "It would be hard to find a man better able to recognize the importance of the values being represented by these groups in balance with competing interests before the NEB hearing." "Mr. Crowe's disqualification," the editorial continued, "is victory in principle and a loss in fact for these groups."

A Canadian Press news agency story from Ottawa at the time of the decision recalled that the Crowe outburst of temper at an early stage in the hearing (mentioned earlier) had done more than wake up witnesses:

"It served notice on the companies that the board wanted all available information on which to base a decision, not just the material the companies chose to provide."

The most passionate reaction came from Charles Lynch, the Southam News Services Ottawa columnist. He first recalled the career of Crowe, which had started with his birth in the small Manitoba town of Rossburn. After earning a Bachelor of Arts degree and serving in World War II, Crowe served in the External Affairs Department from 1947 to 1961. Then he left to become economic advisor to the Canadian Imperial Bank of Commerce, until returning to Ottawa at the request of Prime Minister Pearson in 1967, to take his job as assistant cabinet secretary.

Lynch then wrote that he found it hard to detect "advancement of the public welfare in the Supreme Court order" which removed Crowe from the pipeline hearing. He continued:

To question Crowe's fitness for high office risks conceding administrative power to career bureaucrats unsullied by exposure to the crass world of the marketplace. Crowe is something more than your average mandarin — he has served with distinction in the worlds of international diplomacy, economics, banking, backroom politics, commerce and senior administration. Endlessly curious about just about everything, he has developed a breadth of knowledge that is the very antithesis of the bureaucratic norm.

Lynch noted that Crowe had been a principal advisor to L. B. Pearson during the hectic days of the Suez War, when Pearson won a Nobel Peace Prize for devising a UN peace-keeping force as part of the solution. In the Toronto banking world, Crowe had "soaked up the realities of the marketplace." Serving in the cabinet secretariat of the Privy Council Office under Trudeau, after Pearson's retirement, Crowe had been "one of the few men regarded by Trudeau as an intellectual equal."

"Crowe's sin is that he knows too much about the subject under discussion — the implication is that members of public bodies or tribunals must start with clean slates," Lynch wrote. He saved his best, however, for the last: "The man is more a national treasure than a national menace, and I would trust his views on most matters, including northern development, over those of almost anybody, including the learned judges of the Supreme Court.''

The fascinating (and, for Crowe, haunting) question at the centre of the remarkable case of Marshall Crowe, however, remains unanswered and unanswerable: had Michael Goldie, acting for Canadian Arctic Gas Pipelines, not raised the issue of bias, would any of the other interested parties have done so? There were, in total, 88 persons recognized by the board as representing interested parties in this hearing. As the dissenting Supreme Court justices pointed out, only 5 of these 88 objected, and of those 5, only 3 felt strongly enough to take their objections to court. All of the competing applicants were satisfied that no reasonable apprehension of bias could be entertained.

Or were they all? Although they all went on record in support of Crowe, it was, as others have also observed, one of the applicants which had raised the issue in the first place. There were then only those few tense minutes in the Chateau Laurier Ballroom on the hearing's opening day, waiting to see if someone else would take the issue from there. It was almost certain someone would. And only one would have been enough.

5

THE FINAL
BATTLELINES

The two groups of companies lined up in the final confrontation
with each other could be described as the Arctic Gas group and the
Foothills group. The Arctic Gas group conducts its Canadian
operations primarily from Toronto, and the Foothills group from
Calgary. As has been described in detail, TransCanada PipeLines
and Alberta Gas Trunk Line started out about 1970 as opponents;
they became partners from 1972 to 1974; then split up, and
remained on opposing sides to the end.

1. The Alaskan-Canadian Arctic Gas Project
The proposal by the Arctic Gas group was broadly similar to that
initially filed by Canadian Arctic Gas Pipeline Limited with the
National Energy Board in March 1974. A single pipeline system
would move both Alaskan gas from Prudhoe Bay and Canadian
gas from the Mackenzie Delta to markets in southern Canada and
the United States. With a diameter of 48 inches, the pipe used for
most of this pipeline would be the largest ever employed in North
America for carrying natural gas. The largest to date is 42 inches in
diameter.

The pressure at which the gas would be moved is of even greater
engineering significance. The highest pressure under which gas is
currently moved in pipelines in British Columbia and Alberta is
between 800 and 1,000 pounds per square inch. The Arctic Gas
group's proposed Arctic gas pipeline system would move the gas

at an unprecedented 1,680 pounds per square inch pressure along its permafrost-ridden Northern route.

Following several modifications in the leg between Prudhoe Bay and the Mackenzie Valley, the prime route proposed for this pipeline was across the North Slope of Alaska and the Yukon, never far from the coast of the Beaufort Sea, which is a part of the Arctic Ocean. The line would then cross the northern part of the Mackenzie Delta in the Northwest Territories and connect with a line from Richards Island, in Mackenzie Bay, at a point south of Inuvik. From there the pipeline would run south up the Mackenzie Valley along the east side of the river to a point about 45 miles downstream from Fort Simpson. There it would be buried under the riverbed and cross to the west bank of the Mackenzie, extending from there into Alberta at the northwestern corner of the province and continue south to Caroline, about 75 miles northwest of Calgary.

At that point the pipeline would divide in two and be reduced in size. A branch 42 inches in diameter would continue southeastward; it would connect with the TransCanada pipeline at Empress, on the Alberta border with Saskatchewan due east of Calgary, and continue across the southwestern corner of Saskatchewan to Monchy on the U.S. border. The other branch, 36 inches in diameter, would run south and west through Alberta to a point on the British Columbia border near Coleman, in the Crowsnest Pass. There it would connect with existing but expanded facilities — what would amount to a new pipeline 36 inches in diameter — to complete the journey to Kingsgate, on the British Columbia border with Idaho.

A line 24 inches in diameter would connect the Arctic Gas pipeline system from a point just inside the Northwest Territories southwestward to the existing British Columbia system in the northeast corner of the province.

The Alaskan Arctic Gas Pipeline Company would build and operate the 195 miles of pipeline from Prudhoe Bay to the Yukon border. The Canadian Arctic Gas Pipeline Limited would build the system from there to Coleman, Empress and Monchy — about 2,300 miles altogether. The Westcoast Transmission Company Limited of Vancouver would build the 140-mile connection from the Arctic Gas line to the British Columbia system operated by Westcoast, and the 102 miles of expanded facilities from Coleman to Kingsgate would be built alongside existing pipeline (in a

process pipeliners call looping) by Alberta Natural Gas Company Limited of Calgary, acting as a carrier for gas purchased by Alberta and Southern Gas Company Limited, also of Calgary. Both these companies are subsidiaries of Pacific Gas and Electric of San Francisco.

(Pipeline capacity can be expanded in two ways: by increasing the compression of the gas moving through it and by looping. Increasing the compression becomes progressively more expensive because more gas is needed to fuel the compressor machinery. There is also a limit to the capacity that can be added by compression. Looping means adding a second pipeline parallel to an existing one. This can be done section by section until a complete new line has been built alongside the existing one, a condition pipeliners describe as "looped out.")

The Arctic Gas proposal was actively supported by 15 companies, 4 of which may be described as Canadian. The four Canadian companies are: TransCanada PipeLines Limited of Toronto, Consumers' Gas Company of Toronto, Northern & Central Gas Corporation Limited of Toronto, and Union Gas Limited of Chatham, Ontario. (A fifth Canadian company, the federal government's Canada Development Corporation, ceased to be an active member of the consortium in October 1975, but remains an observer member.) The other 11 companies are either American or Canadian subsidiaries of American companies and of Shell, with Anglo-Dutch parenthood.

The cost estimate on the Alaska section of the Arctic Gas project was about $1 billion, and the section from the Yukon-Alaska border to Caroline, Monchy and Coleman about $10 billion to bring it to full capacity of 4.5 billion cubic feet of gas per day, half of which would ultimately flow from Prudhoe Bay to the United States, and the rest from the Mackenzie Delta to southern Canadian markets. The Westcoast section was estimated to cost about $323 million, and the Alberta Natural Gas "looping" from Coleman to Kingsgate about $74 million. That added up to a total $11.4 billion, according to the April 1977 estimates of Arctic Gas.

If approved, it was estimated that this pipeline would begin delivering Canadian Arctic gas to southern Canadian customers in mid-1982, and Alaskan gas to the U.S. in mid-1983.

2. The Alaska Highway-Maple Leaf Projects.

The proposal by the Foothills group evolved through several stages since its inception as a single 48-inch-diameter pipeline system in 1970. The Foothills group finally supported proposals for two separate pipelines south from the Arctic: one would carry Alaskan gas and the other would carry Canadian gas from the Mackenzie Delta. Each line, though interconnected through the sponsors, was a separate and independent project. Ownership of both lines would be divided by sections among several companies, one American and the rest Canadian.

The Foothills group, for reasons explained earlier, never filed an application for its original single-line proposal. Instead, it proposed, through several separate applications filed with the National Energy Board in March 1975, a pipeline south from the Delta, and in August 1976 a separate pipeline to connect Alaskan gas with the lower United States.

For safety reasons, both pipelines were initially proposed as using conventional pipe 42 inches in diameter, but with transmission pressure pushed to a new high-level of 1,250 pounds per square inch. Because of recommendations made by Federal Power Commission staff, the Foothills group replaced its 42-inch Alaskan gas proposal in March 1977 with a 48-inch-diameter proposal, but with a pressure level of 1,260 pounds per square inch, still well below that proposed by the Arctic Gas group.

The project that would carry Mackenzie Delta gas south came to be known as the Maple Leaf pipeline. It would begin in the same Taglu field on Richards Island as the proposed Arctic Gas line and connect with the existing British Columbia and Alberta pipeline systems by the same general route up the Mackenzie Valley as the Arctic Gas project. Since the existing Alberta system was already connected with the TransCanada pipeline at Empress, the Maple Leaf project would thus connect all existing Canadian markets with gas from the Delta. Total new line: 1,040 miles. Looping: 1,100.

The other project of the Foothills group, the Alaska Highway Project, was also supported by a combination of separate applications before the NEB and the FPC. It would be a pipeline 48 inches in diameter from Prudhoe Bay south to Fairbanks along the already established corridor of the Alyeska oil pipeline, then run southeast along the Alaska Highway route across the Yukon, northeastern British Columbia and Alberta to Caroline. There it would divide into separate branches going to Kingsgate, Empress and Monchy, much as in the Arctic Gas proposal.

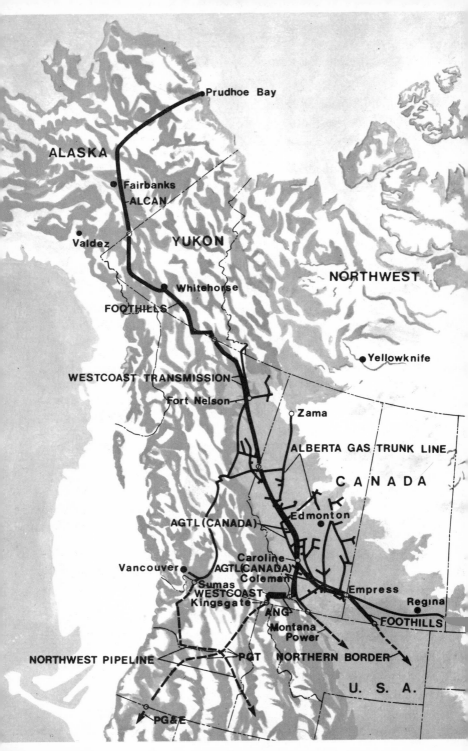

ALASKA HIGHWAY PROJECT

TERRITORIES

TRANSCANADA PIPELINES

innipeg

Emerson

Quebec City

Montreal

Ottawa

GREAT LAKES

Toronto

MIDWESTERN

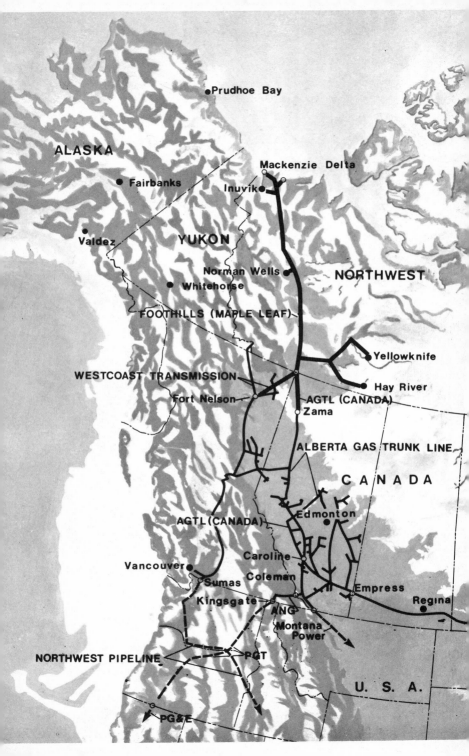

MAPLE LEAF PROJECT

TERRITORIES

TRANSCANADA PIPELINES

Winnipeg
Emerson

Quebec City

Montreal

Ottawa

GREAT LAKES

MIDWESTERN

Toronto

The main companies behind the Foothills group proposals were one Canadian, one majority-owned Canadian and one American. The Canadian company was Alberta Gas Trunk Line Company Limited of Calgary. The majority-owned Canadian company was Westcoast Transmission Company Limited of Vancouver: 34.1 per cent of its equity ownership was held by Pacific Petroleums Limited of Calgary, which in turn was a subsidiary of Phillips Petroleum Limited of the U.S. The British Columbia government held 10.6 per cent of Westcoast Transmission's equity shares and apparently Phillips no longer exercised control over Westcoast. However, should control ever become a serious enough issue to invite direct shareholder action, Phillips could almost certainly have the last word because of its 34.1 per cent ownership exercised through Pacific Petroleums. The American company was the Northwest Pipeline Corporation of Salt Lake City, Utah.

The Northwest Territories section of the Maple Leaf pipeline, 817 miles long and 42 inches in diameter, would be built by a new company formed by Westcoast and Trunk Line, Foothills Pipe Lines Limited of Calgary. From a point 6.5 miles north of the 60th parallel, which forms the northern boundary of British Columbia and Alberta, a new federally-incorporated subsidiary of Trunk Line, Alberta Gas Trunk Line (Canada) Limited, would extend the 42-inch line some 80 miles south to connect with the northern end of the existing Trunk Line system in Alberta. From the same point, Westcoast Transmission would build a 30-inch 140 miles southwestward to connect with its existing British Columbia system.

The Alaska section of the Alyeska Corridor-Alaska Highway pipeline, 731.4 miles long, would be built by a subsidiary of Northwest Pipeline, the Alcan Pipeline Company of Salt Lake. A subsidiary of Foothills Pipe Lines Limited — Foothills Pipe Lines (Yukon) Limited — would build the 512.6 mile section across the Yukon, Westcoast the 543.9 miles across northeastern British Columbia, Trunk Line (Canada) the 806 miles across Alberta, and Foothills (Yukon) the 159.8 miles from Empress across southwestern Saskatchewan to Monchy. Total mileage: 2,750.

The cost estimate for the Maple Leaf Line was about $4.6 billion, and for the Alaska Highway line $7.3 billion — a total of $11.9 billion. The Alaska Highway project was estimated to begin moving Alaskan gas south by October 1981, and the Maple Leaf line by November 1982 or later — if supply, demand and other factors, such as native land claims, indicated a later date.

In announcing the new 48-inch diameter Alaska Highway project on 16 February 1977 (it was filed before the NEB and FPC in March 1977), a Foothills statement noted that "the decision to offer an express-line system exclusively for Alaskan gas rises out of requests for several alternative studies by the National Energy Board counsel hearing the group's present applications" for the joint 42-inch Alaska Highway-Maple Leaf projects. The statement also noted that the 48-inch alternative "meets head-on" the main objections to the two-pipeline proposal by the staff and Judge Nahum Litt of the Federal Power Commission. Both the FPC staff and Judge Litt had found the Arctic Gas proposal, based on 1975 information, superior to both the Alaska Highway-Maple Leaf proposal and the El Paso Alaska when economic and environmental considerations were weighed.

There were other bases for comparing the viability of pipeline projects. These included the terrain through which the pipeline would be laid, the size of the pipe, the working conditions under which the pipeline would be built and other factors (all of which will be examined in a later section). Finally, what counts most, however, is the price to the customer at the delivery end. The same Foothills brief to the NEB in February 1977 contained comparisons of unit delivery costs. For gas pipelines, these are measured by dollars per million BTUs (British Thermal Units) of fuel power delivered. This comparison gave Arctic Gas an edge at Monchy over the combined pipelines for the first two full years of operation — $1.51 per unit against $1.65 in 1983, and $1.55 against $1.64 in 1984. But the advantage would switch in 1985, when the combined pipelines deliver a unit for $1.58 compared to $1.61. The combined pipelines' advantage is seven cents per unit in 1986 and four cents in 1987.

This was on the basis of Arctic Gas material as filed prior to the Foothills brief. Adjusting the Arctic Gas costs upward by 20 per cent, as the brief argued should be done, would put the joint Alaska Highway-Maple Leaf projects at an advantage from 1983 onwards — beginning at $1.65 per unit compared to $1.96, and maintaining a comparable or better spread thereafter.

The Alaska Highway pipeline would ultimately move 2.4 billion cubic feet of Alaskan gas daily from Prudhoe Bay wells. Gas would begin moving by October 1981 and reach full capacity by 1983. The Maple Leaf line would ultimately move the same amount of Mackenzie Delta gas, 2.4 billion cubic feet — based on the initial application comparable to the initial application of Arctic Gas.

3. The El Paso Alaska Project
This project had no direct bearing on whatever decision the Canadian government would finally make about an Arctic gas pipeline, because it would be entirely in United States territory. It proposed, in an application initially filed with the Federal Power Commission in September 1974, to build a pipeline 42 inches in diameter and 809 miles long from Prudhoe Bay along the existing Alyeska oil pipeline corridor to Gavina Point on Prince William Sound. There the gas would be liquefied and shipped via a fleet of 11 tankers 1,900 nautical miles to Point Conception, California. It would then be restored to gas form and shipped to U.S. markets.

4. The Possible Compromise Project
Though it had been little mentioned in the news media, the Federal Power Commission's environmentally-preferred project was not a pipeline along the route proposed by Arctic Gas. It was the Alyeska corridor-Alaska Highway route, with certain variations in design from those proposed in existing applications. Curiously enough, the National Energy Board counsel had shown interest in information about almost precisely the same varied proposal.

The FPC staff drew from the voluminous material submitted by the Arctic Gas, El Paso Alaska, and Foothills groups to put together its own preferred project. The FPC staff worked on this closely with the staff of the United States Department of the Interior over a period of several months. The environmentally-preferred proposal was put forward following what an FPC staff statement on 7 December 1976 called "the most exhaustive study undertaken by the FPC environmental staff to date."

This preference was for a pipeline 48 inches in diameter that would follow the Alyeska corridor to Fairbanks from Prudhoe Bay, and then the Alaska Highway south across the Yukon and British Columbia and into Alberta to Caroline and Empress. The western leg proposed by both competing cross-Canada projects through Coleman and Kingsgate would be dropped as "high risk, uneconomic, unnecessary, and environmentally unsound," according to the FPC Staff Position Brief. And instead of the Maple Leaf line, the FPC staff recommended a pipeline from Richards

Island in the Mackenzie Delta southwestward along the Dempster Highway route to the vicinity of Whitehorse in the Yukon. There the 42-inch Dempster Highway pipeline would connect with the 48-inch Alyeska corridor-Alaska Highway pipeline. The Delta gas would then be fed to Canadian markets through existing Canadian pipeline systems, expanded where necessary.

This combination, the FPC Staff Brief said, "would be environmentally preferable to all three of the applied-for projects." (This was, of course, before the Foothills group's 48-inch Alyeska corridor-Alaska Highway project was filed in March 1977.) The project preferred by FPC staff "could provide the flexibility for expansion not available with the Alcan (42-inch pipeline) proposal, as well as environmental benefits not available with either Arctic Gas or El Paso Alaska."

Again drawing on 1975 information, the FPC staff brief estimated that the cost of its preferred project between Prudhoe Bay and Caroline and Empress would be "in the neighborhood of $6.5 billion." The brief noted that Arctic Gas estimated that the line from Empress to Dwight, Illinois, proposed as part of its project, would cost $1.3 billion. The brief also estimated that the 42-inch Dempster Highway pipeline, capable of carrying 2.4 billion cubic feet of gas daily, would cost "approximately in excess of $2 billion." Also noted in the brief was the fact that, since all these cost estimates were based on July 1975 estimates, all estimates would have to be escalated by the amount of inflation that had occurred since then.

The brief pointed out, too, that all of its conclusions were drawn from 44,584 pages of transcript gathered into 253 volumes; one volume representing each day of FPC hearings into this case. An "enormous record," noted the brief.

The three cost estimates, the brief noted further, added up to a total cost for the FPC staff's preferred project of $10 billion. This was some 16 per cent more than the 1975 cost estimate of the Arctic Gas pipeline proposal, at that time $8.5 billion. "In view of this," the brief concluded, giving economic considerations the nod over all others, "it is still staff's position that such an alternative is not economically viable when compared with the Arctic Gas project." A number of factors in the situation, however, had changed since the brief was issued, not the least of them slower-than-expected finds of proven gas reserves in the Mackenzie Delta area, along with upward revisions of gas available in Alberta, and

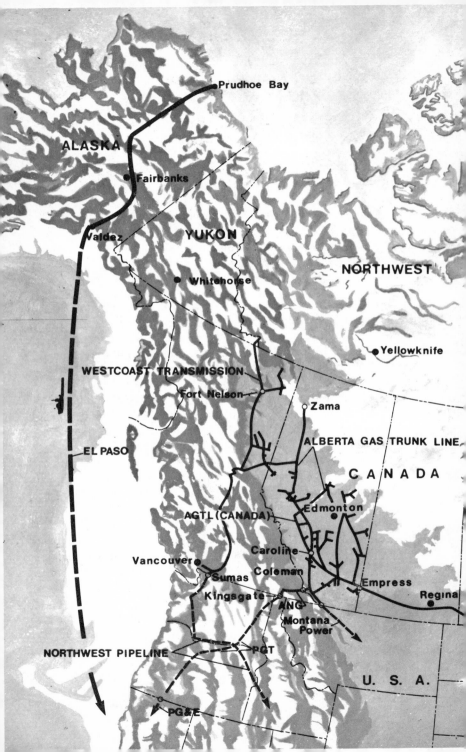

a growing conviction in Canada that no pipeline might be politically possible in the Mackenzie Valley in time to connect Alaskan gas with the lower 48 United States — certainly not as soon as Americans seemed to want this connection completed.

In response to the NEB counsel request for possible alternatives to existing applications, several suggestions were put forward during March 1977. These included reducing the diameter of the Maple Leaf line up the Mackenzie Valley from 42 to 30 inches; building a 30-inch pipeline along the 700-odd mile route of the Dempster and Klondike Highways from Richards Island in the Mackenzie Delta to connect with the Alaska-U.S. express pipeline at Whitehorse, and building a 30-inch line along the Dempster Highway to connect with an express line through Whitehorse by way of Dawson City. The capacity of the 30-inch pipeline, in any of these cases, would be 1.5 billion cubic feet per day — a reduction from a 42-inch line's capacity, reflecting lower-than-anticipated proven reserves to date in the Mackenzie Delta region.

Comparison of Cross-Canada Projects

1. Reserve Estimates:
In his controversial 430-page decision on 1 February 1977, Federal Power Commission Judge Litt included a summary of the Alaskan gas reserve picture. The North Slope of Alaska encompasses an area of 80,000 square miles, extending about 600 miles from the Canadian border up to the Arctic Ocean. Exploration there had only begun and estimates of future potential gas finds varied considerably, but there was general agreement among the various interested parties that proved salable reserves were then about 22 trillion cubic feet. Most of the proved reserves were in the Prudhoe Bay field. They constituted the largest reserves yet discovered in a single field on the North American continent, but represented only about 10 per cent of all proven United States natural gas reserves in 1975. Altogether, the Prudhoe Bay reserves amounted to something more than one year's supply for all U.S. consumers.

The December 1976 staff brief noted that testimony before the FPC indicated that Prudhoe Bay could support a gas sales rate of 2.25 billion cubic feet daily through 1992, and up to 4 billion cubic feet daily after that. The brief also noted that the U.S. Department of the Interior estimated that future reserves in the area could reach

2.5 trillion cubic feet in the Kuparuk formation, and 2.4 trillion cubic feet in the Lisburne formation. The most promising areas of potentially large new gas finds on the North Slope, however, were the Arctic National Wildlife Range and the Alaska section of the Beaufort Sea. Potential reserves in the Wildlife Ranges were in excess of 14.5 trillion cubic feet, and in the adjacent Beaufort and Chukchi sea areas, were 46.5 trillion cubic feet.

That added up to a total potential of new reserves of 65.9 trillion cubic feet — some 30 per cent of known U.S. reserves in 1975. The Atlantic Richfield Company, discoverer of the first Prudhoe Bay well in 1968, estimated then, however, that in the area from Alaska's Brooks Range of mountains out to the 300-foot water depth level offshore, 135 trillion cubic feet of gas might eventually be found; and Mobil Oil Company estimated onshore reserves in the area at potentially 104 trillion cubic feet.

My research in Calgary, Toronto and Ottawa, and reading through mounds of records from FPC and NEB hearings, produced no arguments against the economic viability of a gas pipeline connecting the Alaska reserves to the lower 48 states. However, there was growing evidence of doubt about the viability of any pipeline south from the Mackenzie Delta, on the basis of gas reserves proven there to the end of March 1977.

The way games may be played with reserve estimates, however, is one of the more widely-known secrets of the petroleum industry. The reserve estimates on the competing applications to build a cross-Canada Arctic gas pipeline were, in fact, not all that far apart. Where the divergence became remarkable was in the interpretations that were being given to these estimates. The conflict concerned both reserves in the Mackenzie Delta region and in southern Canada, essentially Alberta.

Canadian Arctic Gas Pipeline, in its 1975 presentation to the National Energy Board, originally estimated reserves in the Mackenzie Delta region at 3.9 trillion cubic feet of gas proven and 2.6 trillion cubic feet probable and possible, for a total of 6.5 trillion. In January 1977, Arctic Gas filed new evidence with the NEB in which the estimate of proven reserves was raised to 5.1 trillion cubic feet, while probable and possible remained at 1.6 trillion, for a total of 6.7 trillion.

Alberta Gas Trunk Line, on behalf of the competing Alaska Highway-Maple Leaf project, had originally estimated in the fall of 1974 that Mackenzie Delta reserves were a total of 7.5 trillion cubic feet (proven, probable and possible) without breaking them down into separate estimates. Their revised estimate in November 1976 reduced the total to 5.7 trillion cubic feet, including proven reserves of 4.9 trillion.

The significant figures in the estimates of both applicants are the proven reserves. Both estimates can be rounded off at 5 trillion cubic feet — exactly two years' worth of Canadian gas requirements at 1975 levels. That year, Canadian consumers used 1.3 trillion cubic feet, exports to the United States under long-standing contracts amounted to 1.0 trillion cubic feet, and fuel for pipeline operations and gas reprocessing took 0.5 trillion, for a total of 2.8 trillion cubic feet.

Neither applicant drew attention to the real significance of the proven reserves figure: it was far below the level of proven reserves considered essential before any pipeline project to move Mackenzie Delta gas south could be justified economically.

Appearing on behalf of the Foothills group before the NEB in Ottawa on 10 December 1976, Robert Blair said that on the basis of currently proven gas reserves in that region, and if no consideration were given to ultimate potential discoveries there, "we could not finance [the line] at the moment." If proven reserves were "in the order of 10 trillion" cubic feet, Blair continued, then "perhaps" the Maple Leaf line as originally conceived could be financed. "It would be tough," he conceded, "but we would like to give it a try."

In his NEB appearance, Blair referred to "information about the ultimate potential" of gas discoveries in Canada's Arctic regions, including islands as yet almost inaccessible to pipelines. The Trunk Line reserve study noted that some 15 trillion cubic feet of gas reserves had been proven to date on the Arctic islands. The study estimated that 287.4 trillion cubic feet — more than one hundred years' worth of Canadian needs at 1975 levels — were believed remaining to be discovered in northern frontier regions, for a total potential of 308 trillion cubic feet.

The Arctic Gas reserve study limited its estimate of potential reserves to the Mackenzie Delta region, onshore and offshore to a water depth of 600 feet. On this basis, Arctic Gas estimated a total of 40 trillion to 60 trillion cubic feet of gas reserves could ultimately be discovered in that region.

The fundamental point for current consideration remained the estimate by both these competing applicants of *proven* reserves in the region of 5 trillion cubic feet. Did that amount make either proposal economically viable? Information material circulated during November 1976 by Canadian Arctic Gas Pipeline stated that a pipeline to carry only Delta gas southward "could not be undertaken until some 16 to 18 trillion cubic feet of gas reserves" had been found in the region. Arctic Gas argued this favoured its pipeline, because it would be backed by the combined reserves of Prudhoe Bay and the Delta region. Another item in this material revealed, however, that proven Delta reserves were still far below Arctic Gas expectations. The volume of Delta gas which the Arctic Gas projected it would deliver to Canadian users during a 22-year period was 14 trillion cubic feet, roughly 9 trillion more than the reserves proven to date.

What potential financial backers of either project were certain to have in mind, when approached to support either project, was the fact that no pipeline had been built anywhere, much less in so difficult an area as the Arctic, until enough proven reserves were found to ensure its economic viability.

Even more to the point, however, were the latest estimates of proven reserves in southern Canada, which had not yet been connected up for existing markets. Trunk Line estimated that there were proven but unconnected reserves in Alberta of 18.8 trillion cubic feet, and that this could rise to 25.5 trillion during actual development. Arctic Gas estimated the proven but unconnected reserves in Alberta at 17.9 trillion cubic feet. Though these estimates were obviously not very far apart, the conclusions which the competing applicants drew from them were pointing in almost directly opposite lines.

"It can be seen from these results," said the Arctic Gas study, "that there is a current deficiency in Canada (occurring at this time in the British Columbia market area) and this deficiency continues to grow with time." The Trunk Line study, however, arrived at this conclusion: "Our supply and requirements study shows that present nonfrontier, producing areas of Canada have the production capability and reserves potential to meet growing domestic requirements and presently approved exports until 1984." How could this dramatic difference in interpretations of roughly the same figures be explained? Easily enough, provided you found the right industry experts.

One of the key words in this explanation is "ownership" — ownership of the gas reserves; or, as this was treated in the Arctic Gas study, "contracts and rate of take." There is no Great Gas Distributor In The Sky automatically matching current proven reserves with current gas demand. Some gas reserves are contracted for immediate delivery, others for delivery over a period of years, usually a maximum of five. Under what is known in the industry as the "take or pay" provision in these contracts, the purchaser must pay for the minimum contracted for, whether it can be marketed or not when the contract date comes due. The purchased but unsold reserves may be left in the ground for up to five years at no extra cost except for the interest on the original purchase price; after five years, however, ownership reverts to the producer. A purchaser with more gas than market thus has an incentive to sell the difference to other customers. Besides this incentive to sell surplus reserves, purchasers may feel the political clout, both direct and indirect, of the government regulatory agencies which can influence their use of reserves they own, but have no immediate market for.

It was against this background that Trunk Line concluded from its reserves study that it did "not see a need to curtail Canadian market growth and there is no supply shortage crisis." The "substantial existing unconnected reserves in Alberta . . . with appropriate action by industry and government, can add substantial production to meet all requirements between now and 1984," its study said.

It was against the same background that the Arctic Gas study found a deficiency already occurring in the markets served by Westcoast Transmission, domestic and export, and a deficiency in markets east of Alberta — primarily Ontario and Quebec — by 1981. It is essential to understand that the Arctic Gas Study "assumed that the contracts on currently connected fields will be maintained in their present form." However, in mid-March 1977, the ownership of Alberta gas reserves had begun to change. Owners of gas destined for future export markets in the United States, in particular, were selling some of their reserves to Westcoast, to help it make up its deficiency.

The Trunk Line reserves study also pointed out that the contracting of gas reserves for anticipated future market demand in particular regions has been "aggressively pursued" in Alberta, particularly by companies delivering to U.S. markets. This, said Trunk Line, "has resulted in an excess of supply, relative to requirements, being contracted." In Trunk Line's opinion, "these excess supply capability volumes should be produced and sold into Canadian markets."

The reason for the different emphasis which each of the competing applicants put on the reserve figures was simple to understand. As a major backer of the proposed Maple Leaf project, Trunk Line was only emphasizing the greater flexibility of the joint proposals put forward by the Foothills group of which it was a member. If the state of both the Delta and southern Canada reserves (not to mention the explosive political issue of unsettled native land claims along the Mackenzie) did not justify early construction of a pipeline up the Mackenzie Valley, there was no urgency to go ahead with the Maple Leaf line. Whether it was built sooner or later or never would have no bearing on construction of the Alaska Highway project, and the undeniably urgent need of the United States for a connection with Prudhoe Bay reserves.

What would happen to the Arctic Gas proposal, if it turned out that there was neither economic justification nor urgent Canadian need for the Mackenzie Delta reserves? Obviously, if the Canadian part of the Arctic Gas project were threatened, the entire project would be thrown into jeopardy. As presented both to the NEB and the FPC, the Arctic Gas project depended equally upon viable amounts of gas from the Canadian Arctic and the Alaskan Arctic. Hence, the Arctic Gas emphasis on the supply-demand picture in southern Canada as reflected in contracts as they stood at the beginning of 1976, instead of as they seemed to be shifting in 1977, to bring about a closer match of current reserves with current Canadian demands.

2. Economic Viability:

A fundamental problem in building a pipeline to move Arctic gas to southern markets would be raising the money to pay for it. And a fundamental dispute between the two cross-Canada applicants was whether the Canadian sections of any of the proposed projects could be financed while retaining equity ownership and control within Canada. They were also in dispute over the extent and manner by which government might, if necessary, help in the financing of an Arctic gas project. Despite the demonstrated shortage of natural gas in the United States and the OPEC's raising of world petroleum prices, the primary determinant for successful financing remained what it always was (as the Federal Power Commission Staff Position Brief issued December 1976 pointed out): "the economic viability of a project."

From the beginning, the Arctic Gas group, represented by the Alaskan–Canadian Arctic Gas projects, had relied for its financing plan upon the economic strength of its own member-companies: producers like Exxon, Shell and Gulf at the northern end, and shippers like TransCanada PipeLines and some of America's biggest pipeline companies at the southern end. The Arctic Gas group steadfastly maintained that only an international consortium, offering equity ownership to both Canadian and American companies would have any real hope of getting the financial backing for this mammoth project — the final cost of it would run around $12 billion by the time both Alaskan and Canadian Arctic gas were moving south. The Arctic Gas group had also insisted from the start that the Canadian section of this pipeline could only be financed as a single corporate entity.

With equal insistence from the beginning, the Foothills group, represented by the Alaska Highway-Maple Leaf projects, relied for its financing plan upon the advantages it saw in having proposed two sequential projects which could each be broken down into individual, separately-owned sections. The Foothills group steadfastly maintained that by building the Alaska Highway pipeline first and the Maple Leaf line 13 to 16 months later, there would be less disruptive demand — on financial markets in Canada, on relatively scarce Canadian manpower skilled in pipelining arts, and on Canadian sources of pipeline materials — than from the single construction effort of Arctic Gas. The group also maintained that the sectional ownership of the lines which it proposed would make the financing of the separate companies' shares in the joint projects less unwieldy than the enormous single amount that the Arctic Gas group would need.

The Arctic Gas group estimated that the major construction on its project would take three years. The Foothills group estimated that each of its two smaller projects would take two years to build, but for the reasons already mentioned, proposed to stretch out their construction over three to three-and-a-half years. Using $12 billion as a reasonable cost estimate for both proposals, Arctic Gas would have to raise the entire amount at once before its project could start. On the other hand, the Foothills group could start on the Alaska Highway project with $7.3 billion, and then start on the

Maple Leaf project 13 to 16 months later with an additional $4.6 billion. The Foothills group argued that this would make financing its proposals less difficult than that of Arctic Gas.

Both groups have amassed distinguished Canadian and American financial experts behind their arguments. By October 1976, the financial challenge appeared to have aroused some headaches for the Arctic Gas group. Their financial experts — Wood Gundy Limited, the Royal Bank of Canada and Toronto-Dominion Bank on the Canadian side; and Morgan Stanley & Company and Citibank of New York on the American side — filed evidence with the National Energy Board that government performance guarantees would probably be needed to secure the financing of an Arctic gas pipeline.

The Foothills group responded by saying that it still believed it would be able to finance its two separate pipelines without government help. However, it argued that if government help did prove necessary, then those sections of the pipeline that could not be financed privately should be built by a crown corporation, with a view to the government's selling this section to private interests if and when the Arctic project proved profitable enough.

Another important difference in the financial plans of the two groups was the degree of Canadian ownership envisaged. Both groups proposed to finance their projects on the basis of 25 per cent equity capital and 75 per cent debt capital in one form or another. The equity capital in the form of common shares is what gives shareholders ownership and control. The Arctic Gas group, as it had from the beginning, still envisaged at least half of the equity shares in its Canadian Arctic Gas Pipeline being sold to Canadians, and the balance to Americans. The Foothills group, as it had from the beginning, still envisaged all the equity shares in both its Alaska Highway and Maple Leaf pipelines being sold to Canadians.

On the question of government back-stopping for any Arctic pipeline, experts for Arctic Gas contended that the project could be financed, but that institutional lenders, such as insurance companies and pension funds likely to buy mortgages and debentures, would probably require some protection against the ''remote'' possibility that costs might rise higher than expected, or that the pipeline might encounter some long-term interruption in service. Robert Blair, appearing before the NEB in December 1976, said that his Foothills group would not request and would ''discourage" and "criticize" a request for government guarantees for a project "to be owned and to be profitable in the private sector."

Blair further stated that no company in Canada could give a guarantee to complete the pipeline, whatever unforeseen costs might develop during construction: "We cannot sign a blank cheque." But before government became involved, an application should be approved and an effort made to finance the project privately. Then if it turned out that the most difficult Arctic sections seemed too risky for private financiers, Blair recommended "that a crown corporation be employed for the portion of the pipeline that could not be financed in the private sector."

"With the government guarantee situation," Blair pointed out, "what you get is a free ride for the private sector." Private companies could put up some of their own money, along with a government guarantee of performance or repayment of borrowed financing capital, "and get a full return to capital or return to common equity" for their money, "while the government takes the risk." As an investor, anyone in the country "would love to have a certain 15 or 16 per cent return to common equity, after income tax, with the government picking up all the down side if anything goes wrong."

"We think it is wrong to seek such a guarantee," Blair said, "not because it is unattractive; because it is too attractive to the investor. . . . If the government is going to take the downs, it also should take the ups."

When it came down to assessing the economic viability of the proposals of either group, the fact emerged that it was simply not possible with any precision. Since the major portion of the Prudhoe Bay and Delta reserves had not been firmly contracted for, neither of the competing cross-Canada applicants had firm market prices available for comparison. This was recognized both by the FPC staff and its law judge Nahum Litt in their findings in favour of the Arctic Gas group in the December 1976 FPC Staff Report:

> In view of the time that will be required to complete any of the projects, we believe that these projected market studies [by the applicants] may no longer be representative of the actual situation. The projected market requirements and anticipated supplies are too speculative to be utilized, particularly for comparative purposes.

Although future markets of individual pipelines might be speculative, the staff report added, "it is apparent that the nation is presently experiencing a natural gas shortage and further, that future supply projections show a continued decline resulting in an even greater shortage." For this reason, despite the absence of gas purchase contracts by which to judge a project's economic viability with accuracy, the FPC staff recommended a trunkline facility to transmit Alaskan gas to the lower 48 states "which would serve all regions of the country with a minimal amount of additional facilities."

Judge Litt, who concluded that the Arctic Gas group's pipeline would "make more gas available sooner, result in less impact on the environment, at less cost to the consumer than either of the competing proposals," drew on the extensive hearing records for assumptions to support comparative prices. He developed price estimates on two bases. One was on the basis of "rolled-in" pricing, by which the Alaskan gas cost would be spread across the entire American system of users. The other was on an "incremental" basis, by which only those customers actually using Alaskan gas would pay its cost.

Where the cost of Alaskan gas was rolled-in — that is, charged to all customers whether their gas came from Alaska or somewhere else — Judge Litt came up with an average price of $1.50 per 1,000 cubic feet, and on an incremental basis an average price of $2.41. Either way, however, a summary of his report declared, "these prices are substantially lower than the price of fuel oil and electricity for all metropolitan areas except California and New York, where there is parity with fuel oil." From this, given the shortage of gas in the United States and the prospect of a steadily worsening one, no one seems to doubt the economic viability of either of the competing projects for moving Alaskan gas to the mainland United States.

However, neither the FPC staff report nor the Litt judgment settled the issue of which project would likely prove to be the better for moving the Arctic gas to the south.

3. Project Design:
Highly placed informants whose identity I have promised to keep confidential have told me that Judge Litt's decision was unlikely to influence the final recommendation of the Federal Power Commission, as it was injudicial and imbalanced, and too eagerly

advocated the Arctic Gas case. In addition, from a Canadian viewpoint, it also almost cavalierly dismissed the issue of native land claims in Northern Canada as not being a serious obstacle to a pipeline, and it seemed based on the assumption that a pipeline connecting the lower U.S. with the Mackenzie Delta as well as Alaska would have a better chance of getting Canadian Arctic gas for export than a line merely connecting the U.S. to Alaska.

The FPC staff report also seemed to cling to a faint hope that Delta reserves might in time justify extending the export of Canadian gas to the U.S., despite the fact that Canada in recent years had been allowing gas export permits to terminate when contracts ran out. It was "very doubtful" that Delta gas reserves would reach a level in future to restore Canadian exports to the U.S. to what they once were; still, the staff concluded that "at best the connection of the Mackenzie Delta reserves will slow down or flatten out curtailment of Canadian exports of gas to the U.S."

The FPC staff stated that "the fundamental underlying conceptual structure" of each of the projects would be the "decisive factor" in selecting the preferred project. This was so because such "key determinants" as economics, environment, engineering, gas supply, financing, tariff and markets were to a large degree predetermined by the initial project design. The choice of a project, the staff concluded, "does not revolve around which market its facilities will serve, but rather which will best provide access to Prudhoe Bay gas for all markets." It had already made clear that it believed sponsors of the Arctic Gas project had chosen "the most logical" route from Prudhoe Bay across western Canada to the central U.S. When the Delta field was added to this, "the choice of the Arctic Gas route becomes overwhelming in its appeal."

Having taken this position, however, the FPC staff recognized that: "It is possible that the Canadian Government will decide it is in Canada's best interests to defer indefinitely into the future consideration of any and all projects south along the Mackenzie River corridor, no matter what the economic consequences for Canada and the United States."

The FPC staff report and the Litt decision listed several other advantages which, in their view, the Arctic Gas group's project had over the Foothills group's Maple Leaf-Alaska Highway projects (according to their original proposals; Foothills altered its proposal after the staff report).

116

The Arctic Gas pipeline would follow the shortest route. A natural corridor, for the most part skirting the mountains, existed between Prudhoe Bay along the Beaufort Sea (of the Arctic Ocean) to the Mackenzie Delta and then south along the Mackenzie River Valley to Alberta.

Because it would be 48 inches in diameter, "a consistent next step in the evolution of high-pressure natural gas pipeline design," the Arctic Gas pipeline would use less fuel to operate than the 42-inch lower-compression lines first proposed by the Foothills group.

Because of its larger design, the Arctic Gas group's pipeline capacity could more easily be expanded if new discoveries of gas were made in the region it served.

Using the single large-diameter high-compression pipeline to serve both Prudhoe Bay and the Delta would provide the cheapest method of delivering American Arctic gas to the American consumers and Canadian Arctic gas to Canadian consumers.

It would be easier to ensure a just allocation of transportation costs for American gas to American consumers and for Canadian gas for Canadian consumers in the single-pipeline system than in the system of co-mingling northern and southern gas through existing pipeline networks, as proposed by the Foothills group.

The Foothills group insisted that its two projects must be treated separately and could not justly be compared together with the Arctic Gas group's single project. The Foothills group argued that their separate pipelines would have separate sources of income, separate security bases, and separate financing — anywhere from a minimum of 13 months apart to several years, depending on Canadian decisions about building any pipeline up the Mackenzie Valley. Although the FPC staff report conceded that "the separability" of the Alaska Highway and the Maple Leaf projects presented problems of comparison with the Arctic Gas project, the staff and Judge Litt decided that from a logical, practical and legal point of view, the two projects must be combined "in attempting to select the superior route." On this basis, the staff report concluded that the combined Alaska Highway and Maple Leaf "system" would deliver gas from Prudhoe Bay and the Mackenzie Delta "in an enormously inefficient way."

The staff report complained that the Foothills group's own cost exhibits showed that using Westcoast Transmission's pipeline system through British Columbia was "significantly more expensive" than using the Trunk Line system through Alberta would be, and that the Alaska Highway-Maple Leaf projects were "much costlier" than the Arctic Gas project "for both the U.S. and Canadian consumers." It called the Foothills group's methods of allocating gas shipment costs between American and Canadian consumers "inequitable" and "unsupported," described its capital cost estimates as "highly questionable," and concluded that as a result the group's projected unit costs were not only higher but also "highly suspect."

As for Judge Litt, he advised that the Alaska Highway project, on the basis of the enormous record of evidence heard before him, had not the support of "even the possibility that a certificate [of approval] could be granted it. Its design is clearly neither efficient nor economic since the pipeline is undersized." In an April 1977 statement, however, the FPC staff disagreed, saying that they were "Not at all clear" why the judge had taken this position.

Litt made the same point about sales contracts for Prudhoe Bay gas as did the FPC staff report. These constituted "an essential" but missing ingredient in the normal regulatory process. This lack showed that the 13 producers with interest in Prudhoe Bay reserves were waiting to see what the market would bear when their gas finally was connected with southern markets. "They are mainly dickering over price," complained Litt. The national interest "lies somewhere below their own economic interest."

Both Litt and the FPC staff also agreed that the most significant environmental concern heard by the American agency was directed at the fact the Arctic Gas group's pipeline would cross the 14,000-square-mile Alaskan Wildlife Range. Its right-of-way would need about 2,650 acres on the Alaska section. However, the staff report allowed that its environmental analysis showed that "there are undesirable aspects associated with each project." The staff's environmental preference was for the Alaska Highway route — but not if it included the Maple Leaf pipeline system. In that case, the Arctic Gas route was environmentally as well as economically preferable. Still, either of the projects was considered "environmentally acceptable," presuming mitigating measures were adequately implemented and successfully enforced.

Based on their substantial resources of experience in pipeline design and construction experience, the companies in the Foothills group initially proposed projects with one marked difference from the Arctic Gas project: a lower pipeline operating pressure. The 42-inch Maple Leaf line was designed to operate at 1,250 psi because this was closer to the actual experience of its backers with 42-inch lines in British Columbia and Alberta — though the pressure would be a substantial increase from the pressure of between 800 and 1,000 psi currently used in lines in southern Canada. In the 48-inch Alaska Highway line proposed by the Foothills group, the pressure would only go up slightly, to 1,260 psi.

On the other hand, the entire plan of Arctic Gas to build a pipeline 48 inches in diameter and destined under full power to operate at 1,680 pounds per square inch pressure was based on models, not actual experience.

The Foothills group was convinced the higher-pressure Arctic Gas project would be unreliable and unsafe in design, especially for the kind of difficult terrain through which it would be built.

4. Rebuttal:

After the FPC staff report was issued in December 1976 and the Litt decision in February 1977, a substantial amount of complex material was filed with both the Federal Power Commission and the National Energy Board, intended to rebut their findings in favour of the Arctic Gas pipeline project. One of these was an inch-thick brief to the FPC from the American partners in the Foothills group, Alcan Pipeline Company and its parent, the Northwest Pipeline Corporation, both of Salt Lake City, Utah. The rebuttal brief was filed with the blessing of their Canadian partners in the Alaska Highway project: Foothills Pipe Lines (Yukon) Limited, Westcoast Transmission Company Limited, Alberta Gas Trunk Line Limited and Alberta Gas Trunk Line (Canada) Limited. Another brief was a "Comparative Risk Assessment" of the Arctic Gas and Alaska Highway projects, done for Foothills Pipe Lines by Lemberg Consultants Limited of Oakville, Ontario. Between these two documents, all of the serious objections to the FPC staff and Litt findings seemed to be reasonably summarized.

The Alcan brief to the FPC first listed the many areas in which uncertainty on critical issues about either project remained, drawing from the Litt decision to do so.

Before natural gas can be shipped through a pipeline to consumers, it must be taken from wells and processed in production plants at the sending end. As the Alcan brief charged:

> There is no operating plan or even a production unit agreement in existence for the Prudhoe Bay field. As a result, while deliverability estimates have been presented which establish the outer boundaries of the potential deliverability of the field, no proposed deliverability schedules could be presented or tested. No meaningful finding can be made on the rate of build-up of deliverability in the initial years of gas production, and no supportable finding on the proper size for the pipeline can be made until additional information is available. . . . The wellhead price of the Prudhoe Bay gas is not known, the identity and location of the purchasers of the gas are not known, and it is not possible to know at this time even the percentage split of the Prudhoe Bay volumes between purchasers in the East and Midwest, and purchasers in the West. . . . The lack of knowledge of the wellhead price, the gas processing and gathering costs, and the markets proposed to be served also makes definitive findings on marketability difficult.

Furthermore, the brief noted: "Fundamental safety and reliability issues related to pipeline design have not yet been resolved" by U.S. or Canadian agencies.

Because of all these uncertainties, the Alcan brief declared that the FPC, in choosing the project to recommend to President Carter, should concentrate on the route proposed. The pipeline route would determine the environmental impact, in large part the economics of transporting Alaskan gas to American consumers, and the vulnerability of a project to schedule delays, cost overruns, and interruptions of service — the major risks.

The brief recalled that the Arctic Gas pipeline route was conceived when Delta gas was thought to be available, along with Prudhoe Bay gas, for delivery to the U.S., but Canadian policy had changed to reserve Delta gas for Canadian needs. This, plus "considerable growing doubt concerning the time frame in which Canada would permit any pipeline to be built through the Mackenzie Valley," were the factors that had led to proposing the Alaska Highway project. It had been conceived as providing "a reasonable alternative" to the Arctic Gas project for moving Alaskan gas south. The Alaska Highway route would remove the environmental and other pitfalls evident in the Arctic Gas route.

120

The Alcan brief described the Litt decision as "vitiated by pervasive bias" against Alcan and "an advocate's effort to sell the Arctic Gas proposal." One item used as evidence of this was the Litt decision's claim —"a glaring example of bias"— that Arctic Gas had done the "primary" research undertaken in the area of permafrost and frost heave problems. "In fact, many of the Arctic Gas studies praised by the Judge were conducted by co-sponsors of the Alcan project," the brief claimed, and it went on to detail some past history:

Alberta Gas Trunk Line was the operator of the original Gas Arctic Systems group and as such initiated and supervised the extensive permafrost and frost heave studies which were conducted by that group in 1970, 1971, and 1972. AGTL operated the test facilities at Prudhoe Bay and Norman Wells during that time, and its engineers constituted the bulk of the technical staff.

The brief further pointed out that Trunk Line had continued as an active participant in the studies in 1973 and 1974 as a member of the amalgamated Gas Arctic Northwest Project Study group: "Thus, a significant portion of the basic Arctic Gas engineering work is the product of AGTL engineers." In addition, AGTL had a proprietary interest in all information, data and studies generated by these study groups prior to its withdrawal from the consortium in September 1974. All of this material was available for use in the design of all segments of the Alaska Highway project. And since September 1974, the Canadian sponsors of the project had continued these design studies, both for the Alaska Highway and the Maple Leaf projects.

The Alcan brief then charged that Judge Litt's "error" in choosing to ignore this and other substantial evidence of its geotechnical research was "all the more egregious" when viewed in the context of his praise for the other applicants. The record showed, for example, that Arctic Gas had soil samples from "a scant" 64 bore holes over the 195 miles of its proposed route across the North Slope of Alaska to the Yukon border, including a 30-mile stretch over which no soil samples had been taken. Alcan, on the other hand, had drilled 30,000 bore holes where its route was adjacent to the Alyeska oil pipeline, and some 200 more had been drilled by Alcan and 100 more by Foothills Pipe Lines on the portion of the route following the Alaska Highway route in Alaska and the Yukon, plus the results of many prior drilling programs along the highway. Nor was Arctic Gas progressing with its investigations in this area; it proposed to do no more soil boring whatsoever in Alaska until at least the summer of 1977.

"Thus," said the brief, "if Alcan's preliminary geotechnical studies are inadequate, Arctic Gas' studies of soil conditions in Alaska are virtually non-existent." In view of the "amazing lack" of geotechnical research by Arctic Gas, how could Judge Litt have failed to mention this and yet find that Alcan's designs —"which clearly showed that it had conducted more geotechnical investigations and had more information than did Arctic Gas"— lacked the necessary preliminary studies for evaluation?

The brief also attacked Litt's evaluation of the financial feasibility of the Alaska Highway project.

Although Alcan's total financial requirements are substantially less than those of Arctic Gas, and although the Alcan and Maple Leaf projects, taken together, require a level of funding approximately equal to Arctic Gas, the Judge finds Arctic's financial plan feasible, whereas Alcan's is subject to "serious doubt."

The Judge "readily admits," the brief continued, that this doubt arose out of his treating the Alaska Highway and the Maple Leaf projects as a single project and assuming that both would be financed simultaneously. This would "vitiate" the financibility of the project, the judge had found. "Whatever the merits of this argument," the brief said, "the Alcan financial advisers and policy witnesses made clear at the hearing that an overlap between Alcan and Maple Leaf financing would not in fact occur." The Litt decision readily admitted that the relative capital requirements of the projects were distorted in its finding; it listed the estimated cost of the Alaska Highway project in 1976 dollars and lumped this together with the estimated cost of the Maple Leaf project, while using the Arctic Gas estimate in 1975 dollars. On an unescalated basis, the brief pointed out, the Alaska Highway project had the lowest capital requirements — $6.42 billion, compared to Arctic Gas' $8.52 billion.

The brief also asserted that no unescalated cost figures were available for the Maple Leaf project. However, taking the Alaska Highway and Maple Leaf projects together and comparing them to Arctic Gas on an escalated basis, including a new line to be built in the lower 48 states, produced these estimates: Alaska Highway-Maple Leaf $14.6 billion, and Arctic Gas $14.3 billion. Though the brief did not raise it, an obvious question was unanswered: if one group could raise such an amount, why could not another?

The brief described as "presumptuous and uninformed" Judge Litt's "attempt to treat as frivolous the extremely serious problems faced by Canada in its efforts to preserve the rights of the indigenous population of the Mackenzie Delta and the Mackenzie Valley." It referred particularly to the comment in the Litt decision that "it is unlikely that native claims will significantly modify the Canadian Government's energy decisions." These claims were in fact "extremely significant" for two reasons. They would undoubtedly affect the timing of any Mackenzie Valley pipeline, and it was "highly unlikely" that any Mackenzie Valley pipeline could be financed until they were "substantially resolved."

As evidence, the brief quoted a principal financial witness for Arctic Gas, J. R. LeMesurier, in an appearance before the National Energy Board on 23 November 1976:

> . . . [I] think that lenders and public equity holders are going to have to be satisfied that the land claims have either been resolved, or that any risk to the project from lack of complete resolution of the land claims has been reduced to a minimum acceptable level. It may be some basic settlement has been reached, it may be that there are some loose tag ends, it may be the federal government has the power to resolve them, and it may not be necessary that everything has to be finally settled, but lenders have to be satisfied that there will not be a serious impact on the project if they have not been fully resolved at the time of financing.

Judge Litt's dismissal of the native claims as "a mere administrative problem which can be extinguished by the Canadian Government, if necessary," the brief asserted, was a legalistic approach reflecting "an appalling insensitivity to the problem." It was a question of "affording fair treatment to the social, environmental, and economic needs of a substantial portion of the population which will be directly affected by a major construction project," the brief went on, "across the lands which they have occupied for centuries and which they claim as their own. The Judge's suggestion that Canada would only use the native claims issue as an excuse for not approving a joint facility is a vulgar and tasteless affront to the Government of Canada."

In the introduction to its "Comparative Risk Assessment" of

the Arctic Gas and Alaska Highway projects, dated at Oakville on 23 February 1977, Lemberg Consultants Limited complimented its client, Foothills Pipe Lines, for having "the courage . . . to undertake a study whose findings and possible impact on their project would not be known until the study was completed." The Lemberg assignment was to develop "a rational basis" on which to assess the relative risks faced by the projects. The consultants produced a basis for comparing the relative chances of each project completing its construction as planned, reasoning that the project most likely to deviate from its basic construction plan would run the greater risk of cost overruns and delays. The probability of each project being completed according to its basic construction plan was deduced from four risk areas:

1. Risks which might impede a go-ahead for the project.
2. Risks which might affect a start of construction.
3. Risks which might alter the length of a construction season.
4. Risks which might degrade planned productivity per working day.

The Lemberg report noted that, although the Arctic Gas route was shorter than the Alaska Highway route, the Arctic Gas pipeline involved construction and operating technology untested anywhere.

It would also be built through hundreds of miles of difficult Arctic terrain, where there had been no previous construction of any kind. "Traditionally, new technology, unfamiliar environments, and a large scale relative to previous projects are exactly the ingredients for significant cost overruns," the report observed. "Experience in North America with big, one-time construction projects has been that they normally cost much more than their original projections."

The Alaska Highway route was different on two points. It would follow existing transportation corridors where construction conditions were less extreme and better known, and it was likely to encounter less intense environmental opposition because it had fewer river crossings, did not invade the Arctic Wildlife Range, and followed corridors already affected by development.

Using the probability bases already mentioned, the Lemberg assessment concluded that the chances of completing the Alaska Highway route according to the base construction plan were from nine to four hundred times better than for the Arctic Gas route. The report attributed the primary differences to these factors:

1. The Alaska Highway project would not depend on Canadian government guarantees, Delta gas reserves, or gas pricing mechanisms in Canada, whereas Arctic Gas would.
2. The Alaska Highway project had better access to construction sites, proven pipe suppliers (for its 42-inch diameter, but not its 48-inch proposal), and fewer impediments to obtaining right-of-way than Arctic Gas.
3. The Alaska Highway project proposed conventional summer and winter construction (on gravel pads in Alaska) and thus would not be sensitive to tundra opening and closing dates determined by weather and environmental factors, or to severe weather hampering production or causing extra operations to become necessary.
4. The Alaska Highway project planned conventional construction methods, whereas Arctic Gas plans would depend on the development of a "super ditcher" and other untried equipment.
5. The Alaska Highway project planned a two-year construction period, whereas Arctic Gas would take three years, thus exposing its project to an additional year of risks.

This brings us to a final basis for comparing the Alaska Highway and Arctic Gas proposals.

5. Project Flexibility:

The virtues of the Arctic Gas proposal have already been listed, as drawn from the works of the FPC staff and Judge Litt. Not surprisingly, they were not applauded in the Alcan brief filed on 1 March 1977 with the FPC. The brief maintained that the original Alaska Highway proposal for a pipeline 42 inches in diameter, contrary to the FPC staff arguments, would provide "substantial flexibility" to adjust to changes in gas supply and deliverability conditions on the North Slope of Alaska, and to market demands in the lower United States. The 48-inch alternative put forward in March 1977 by Alcan in the U.S. and its Foothills group partners in Canada indicated a willingness to provide "additional system flexibility if appropriate regulatory authorities require it," the brief said.

The preferred project was still the 42-inch proposal. It was "optimally-sized to handle the volumes which are likely to be available from Alaska throughout the life of the project." The brief went on:

> Thus, at its design volumes of 2.4 billion cubic feet per day, the Alcan 42-inch system has expansion capability, without the addition to any facilities, of 20 per cent above the anticipated maximum daily volume of 2 billion cubic feet. And Alcan has demonstrated that its 42-inch system can be expanded without looping to an average daily volume of approximately 2.9 billion cubic feet (3.1 billion cubic feet on a peak day) — an expansion capability 45 per cent above the expected volume of 2 billion cubic feet.

And, of course, the Alaska Highway system, like the Arctic Gas system, could be expanded further through incremental looping or a combination of looping and higher compression. What it came down to, finally, was whether a pipeline should be built on the basis of known facts about gas reserves, or a combination of these facts and reasonable expectations for larger finds in the future. The Alaska Highway 42-inch project would tie in with existing pipeline systems in Canada which would require looping and added compression to increase capacity as Arctic gas volumes built up. An express line 48-inch alternative or the Arctic Gas project would incorporate pre-built capacity for future expansion.

The Arctic Gas project, however, would incorporate pre-built expansion up to 50 per cent, dependent upon Mackenzie Delta gas deliveries for justification. (This dependence upon gas from the 15,000-square-mile Delta was noted in the Litt decision.) There was little dispute over the amount of recoverable reserves at Prudhoe Bay, but there was no such agreement on the size of Delta reserves, which, an FPC summary of Litt's report said, "are critical since the Arctic Gas proposal is directly dependent on delivery of at least 1 billion cubic feet a day the first year of operation."

This, then, concludes the summary of economic and technical pros and cons about the competing projects — a summary of issues in these areas upon which the governments of Canada and the United States finally had to make their decisions. The environmental, ecological and socio-economic, or human, issues are examined in following chapters.

6

ENVIRONMENTAL PROBLEMS

The thoroughness and extensiveness of the ecological and environmental studies carried out since 1970 by the Foothills and Arctic Gas groups is impressive, undeniable, and certainly without precedent in past resource development projects. Virtually all of the basic studies were launched before and during the time that both the applicant groups were united in the Gas Arctic/Northwest Project Study Group. The Foothills group continued to make use of study material available to it up to the time it left the merger in September 1974, plus other material gained in additional studies of its own, and those of Arctic Gas, government agencies and other sources.

The basic studies fell under nine main headings: terrain, which included topography, bedrock geology, surface geology and permafrost conditions; climate, including air masses, weather systems, duration of daylight, temperature variations, wind velocities, snow cover, ice-fog, blowing snow and precipitation; hydrology, especially drainage characteristics of the routes; archaeology, including investigations already done along the routes, prehistory of native peoples, historic native land and resource use patterns, and a list of known archaeological sites; aesthetics of the landscape; land-use patterns and land-use capability; vegetation types and methods for preserving and restoring; aquatic systems, including streams and lakes and their uses by fish, birds, and mammals.

The studies were conducted over the years by a variety of highly qualified biological consultants and other experts in such diverse fields as geotechnics, hydrology, archaeology and landscape architecture. The persons from these disciplines often worked with pipeline engineers on interdisciplinary studies, to bring an element of environmental consideration into pipeline planning never applied so extensively to the planning of any previous pipeline project.

In its basic environmental statement to the NEB, Canadian Arctic Gas Pipeline Limited explained why this painstaking attention has been paid to factors almost always ignored by resource developers in the past. "Society's growing awareness of the importance of natural resources and of man's capacity to change the environment is one of the unique developments of this decade," the statement said by way of introduction. "In both the political and economic fields, efforts are being made to evaluate environmental factors and to place them in proper priority." The statement noted that in 1970 the Canadian government proclaimed priorities for Northern development "listing environmental protection second only to human welfare."

"Because vast areas of the Northwest Territories and Yukon Territory are still virtually wilderness," the statement declared, "there is a unique opportunity to develop an integrated plan for the rational management of northern natural resources." With this in mind, Arctic Gas "has accepted the responsibility of satisfying the concerns of the public and Government by undertaking the environmental research needed to design, construct and operate the proposed gas pipeline in a way that would cause minimum disturbance to northern ecosystems."

There were three main objectives of the basic studies. One was to determine the existing environmental setting through which the proposed pipeline would be built. Another was to determine the nature and duration of environmental changes that might result from building and operating the pipeline. The final objective was then to devise procedures for incorporating biological knowledge into engineering construction and operation plans "to provide the highest possible degree of protection of the environment."

The studies began with a thorough search of existing literature about wildlife, fisheries and vegetation in the proposed project region. This included examining unpublished material in university libraries, which led to the discovery that "there was still a

128

general paucity of environmental data available." Much more general information was needed on an inventory of resources in the region, as well as more sophisticated information on the relationship between physical factors of the environment such as soil characteristics and the growth of vegetation. The weather conditions in the forest areas were little known, so field observations of weather, solar energy flux and hydrological regimes were included in environmental programs.

Pipeliners had never before included among their feasibility studies reports with titles such as the following taken from a Foothills group list:

— "Indices of Aquatic Furbearer Habitat Along the Proposed Pipeline."
— "Carnivore Populations of the Mackenzie Valley and Potential Impacts of Gas Pipeline Development."
— "Ungulate Surveys in the Mackenzie Valley."
— "Eagles, Hawks, and Falcons of the Mackenzie Valley and Their Relation to Pipeline Development."
— "Waterfowl of the Mackenzie Valley and Their Relation to Pipeline Development."
— "Special Studies Related to Birds of the Mackenzie Valley and the Potential Effects of a Gas Pipeline."
— "Acquatic Systems Along the Proposed Foothills Pipe Lines Ltd. Route."
— "A Summer Reconnaissance of Mammal Distribution Along the Proposed Pipeline Route."

Studies of the pipeline's potential impact on the ecology ranged from simulating the sound of compressor stations at test facilities along the proposed route, to tests in laboratories under rigidly controlled conditions. Environmental information was a part of the pipeline design input from the beginning, but there were times, the Arctic Gas brief said, when "certain environmental recommendations were not entirely compatible with engineering, geotechnical or reasonable economic requirements. Indeed, occasionally there were conflicting optimal requirements for various components of the plant and animal communities."

When this happened, management settled the incompatibility with a "reasonable compromise" based on a review of all the pertinent social environmental and engineering factors and recommendations. "In each case," the brief emphasized, "the goal was to restrict the overall potential environmental impact to a minimum.''

A sceptic reading this could scarcely be blamed for immediately becoming suspicious. Would not a pipeline consortium's management, true to ancient capitalist tradition, settle any incompatibility between environmental and ''reasonable economic'' concerns in favour of the economic? In this area of ethical measurement, the Arctic Gas group gave more reason for suspicion than the Foothills group. The experience of the Environmental Protection Board is probably the most telling case in point — a case touched upon in an earlier chapter.

The EPB was set up in September 1970 by Alberta Gas Trunk Line. Some pains were taken to ensure that the board enjoyed full independence, so that its judgments on environmental issues in the proposed pipeline region would not only be objective, but would also be seen to be free. Its mandate was to make studies and publish its findings about the potential impact of the pipeline on northern ecology and environment without any editing or revising by its sponsor, whose only control was over the size of the budget.

One of the first concerns of the new management of the study group produced by the 1972 amalgamation of the Northwest and Trunk North groups was this uncustomary freedom of expression, including critical expression, which the board had been given by Trunk Line.

On 8 February 1973, less than a year after the amalgamation brought the board under control of the new Gas Arctic/Northwest Project study group, stories appeared in the news media when the board announced that its operating procedures had been changed. Thereafter, the sponsor, not the board, would decide what field investigations the board made. The board, said its members (who were specialists in Arctic research and environmental science), believed that this shift in control need not affect the autonomous nature of the board; it would continue to express its opinions openly without prior editing by the sponsor. By the fall of 1975, however, the sponsors had refused to finance a board study of route changes made by Arctic Gas, and in January 1976, the board announced it was folding up.

The board had earlier declared that its studies of routes proposed indicated that, if reasonable precautions were taken, the environmental impact could be held to acceptable levels. ''We were not, and still are not in a position to say that this applies to the new route," the board's farewell statement said, "and so our conclusions regarding over-all impact and acceptability may be invalid."

The Dempster Highway Alternative Route

Like the environmental staff of the Federal Power Commission, the staff of the Berger Mackenzie Valley Pipeline Inquiry indicated a preference in projects. In their October 1976 report of "Commission Counsel Submissions," the Berger Inquiry staff said that the Foothills group's proposal for a pipeline along the Alyeska corridor to Fairbanks and then along the Alaska Highway "offers environmental advantages" over either of the routes proposed by the Arctic Gas group. If this Alaska Highway line were built, the Berger staff report said, repeating what the FPC staff had urged, "then the Dempster Highway route should be assessed and reviewed, on a priority basis, as an alternative to the Mackenzie Valley route for transport of gas (and as an energy transportation corridor) southward from the Mackenzie Delta."

The staff report noted that the Berger Inquiry had heard precious little about the Dempster Highway route and the impact which a pipeline along it might have. Despite the very limited information available, the report observed that "its location along an already developed transportation route is an indication that it may have advantages, both environmentally and perhaps for native people."

Aside from Berger's own report, the most recent non-partisan analyses of the environmental and ecological issues are those produced by the FPC and Berger Inquiry staffs. The analysis of the issues that follow was drawn largely from those sources, but included material from both the groups competing for a cross-Canada pipeline approval.

Before going into that, however, a few words about the Dempster Highway. It was one of the lasting consequences of the 1958 "Northern vision" of then Prime Minister John Diefenbaker. Spurred in part by petroleum exploration and the first oilwell drilling in the Yukon, the highway's initial route survey was carried out that year, and the first 30 miles of highway were built in 1959. The Dempster Highway begins at Mile 88 on the Klondike Highway, about 25 miles southeast of Dawson City. (The Klondike Highway follows a jagged semi-circle northwest from Whitehorse to Dawson City; then the road curves southwest into Alaska at Sixtymile, and goes on to rejoin the Alaska Highway at Tetlin Junction.) From Mile 88, at the confluence of the Klondike

and North Klondike Rivers, the Dempster route runs northeasterly through the north-central Yukon and into the Northwest Territories just south of the Mackenzie Delta. It will connect by ferry across the Mackenzie River with the northern segment of the Mackenzie Highway at Arctic Red River to carry on to Inuvik. Plans include an extension to Tuktoyaktuk, northeast of Inuvik on the Arctic coast. The Dempster Highway is the first permanent road connection between southern Canada and the Arctic, the only highway in a 250,000-square-mile area.

The highway follows the overland trail between the Yukon and Peel Rivers said to have been used for centuries by the Kutchin Indians. From 1905 to 1917, the route was patrolled by the Dawson patrol of the Northwest Mounted Police by dog team. The highway was named after Mountie corporal W. J. D. Dempster, who led a famous patrol over the route in 1911 to find the frozen bodies of an earlier patrol lost near Fort McPherson.

One of the reasons for the Berger Inquiry staff's recommendation against any Prudhoe Bay gas pipeline across the northern Yukon, whether along Arctic Gas' preferred coastal route or its second-choice island route, was an environmental one. The staff concluded that there would be "major difficulties" in protecting the environment. Similar objections were raised against any pipeline crossing the Mackenzie Delta. Most of the "really important concerns" about mammals, birds, fish and the protection of the environment, the staff report noted, were brought before the Berger Inquiry in connection with the various route options for a pipeline from Prudhoe Bay to the Mackenzie Valley.

"All of the routing options involve major environmental concerns," the staff report declared. "In particular the coastal cross-Delta route, which is the present prime route of Arctic Gas, is the focus of many critical concerns over environmental impact." There were also ecological concerns. The material from which the Berger and FPC staffs drew their information included primarily the extensive studies, going back to 1970, financed by both applicant groups, the Arctic Gas and Foothills. There is space here only for a relatively brief summary of all the information now available as a result of these studies.

Permafrost
In its original announcement, the Northwest Project Study Group said that an Arctic gas pipeline test facility would be built some-

where along the Mackenzie River during the summer of 1970. Williams Brothers Canada Limited of Calgary were assigned to conduct the research, "with particular emphasis on ecological and environmental considerations." A major one of these considerations was how to build a pipeline through permafrost. The particulars of the permafrost challenge were described in a paper delivered to a Chicago petroleum engineering symposium in April 1971 by Lee G. Hurd of the Northwest Group's Calgary-based office.

Hurd said that his paper dealt only with those challenges to technology peculiar to an Arctic pipeline. He continued:

> Behind the most significant of these challenges is the existence of permafrost which will be encountered throughout nearly half the pipeline route. The simple definition for permafrost is "permanently frozen soil," but little else about it should be called simple. Permafrost may be continuous or intermittent. It may be detrimental, as is the case where the frozen soil is fine silt with a high "ground ice" content (ranging up to 60 or 80 per cent), or non-detrimental, where the soil is well-drained sand or gravel. In addition, ice lenses occur frequently, ranging in thickness to over 50 feet and in area to two or three city blocks. Vertical ice wedges are also common and are the cause of the "ice wedge polygon" surface patterns which cover large areas in the Arctic.

Hurd's paper also described with precision the risks of erosion posed by the permafrost:

> Overlying the permafrost is a thin "active layer" of vegetation, which grows in short bursts during the Arctic summer. This organic material provides remarkably good thermal insulation for the permafrost beneath it.
>
> In the areas near the coast of the Arctic Ocean, the permafrost is usually quite stable so long as the thin layer of organics is left intact to maintain the very delicate thermal balance between earth and atmosphere. Disturbance of this vegetation, if it overlies detrimental permafrost, is followed the next summer by deterioration of the permafrost. The disturbance can be and often is caused naturally by the formation of a pond, which is a better conductor of heat than a drained, vegetated area, and the result is thermokarst subsidence — the pond often becomes a small lake.

Of more concern to the pipeliner is the frequent consequence of man-made disturbance of the vegetation by crushing under vehicular traffic or by its removal in search of solid ground. The result of such disturbance can be both thermokarst subsidence and, if the terrain is sloping, thermal erosion. The latter term describes a process of progressive melting of the ground ice and the runoff or erosion of the resulting slurry. The thermal erosion process can be started by a track only inches in depth and over a few summers can open a ditch many feet deep.

Hurd was aware, as is anyone else who has ever flown low over the Arctic tundra, that this has been a consequence of early seismic explorations in the North. The tracks of seismic vehicles travelling on the tundra in an earlier time, before concern for Arctic ecology had reached the intensity of today, can now often be seen from the air as deep trenches or even gullies.

Hurd's paper further pointed out that construction practices in the face of these kinds of problems must include either repair of the protective insulating layer covering permafrost or, where practical, routing the pipeline around such areas. He also noted that the problems were not the same for gas pipelines as for oil pipelines. Carrying hot oil, as the Alyeska line would, meant mounting the pipe above ground on piles (frozen into the permafrost) that would not conduct the 170-degree F. heat from the flowing oil. Another way of insulating the hot pipeline from the permafrost, shown by field tests at Inuvik and elsewhere to be effective, was to build the line in the centre of a gravel berm.

The Northwest Group believed there was a simpler solution available to the gas pipeline engineer. It proposed to bury the line and chill the gas to a temperature that would not melt the permafrost through which it passed. To confirm the feasibility of this approach, Williams Brothers was assigned to build a full 48-inch diameter Arctic pipeline test facility.

A site on the west bank of the Mackenzie River, at its junction with the Mountain River between Fort Good Hope and Norman Wells, was chosen for the test facility, but only after six other locations had been examined. The site was chosen because it offered a variety of different soil types concentrated in a relatively small area. Permafrost in the general area was about 300 feet deep. The "active layer," the organic material which thaws in the short, warm summer, was not too thin. Substantial quantities of gravel were available from a source where excavation of it would not be harmful to fish life. There was reasonably convenient access for the many tons of equipment and materials which had to be delivered to it.

The test facility which Arctic Gas built at the river junction was similar to test facilities that Foothills built, one on the Alaska North Slope overlooking Prudhoe Bay, one at Norman Wells up the Mackenzie River from the Foothills' site, and a small one operating as part of Alberta Gas Trunk Line's existing pipeline system in a northern part of the province.

The Arctic Gas facility consisted of five 500-foot-long sections of 48-inch diameter pipe. Four were buried in the permafrost, each in a different type of soil. The fifth was partly above ground, mounted on pilings set deep into the frozen soil; it also passed through the active layer into permanently frozen fine silt with high ice content. The five sections were connected to compressor units and heating and refrigeration equipment to simulate actual pipeline operation under a variety of circumstances. Complex instruments were hooked to the sections to monitor the results.

A little-publicized disaster which struck Arctic Gas in the fall of 1976 stemmed from another major difference in design between the competing projects. Their design information, drawn from several years of model research into the effect of frost-heave on pipelines was discovered by Arctic Gas to have been badly affected by a faulty diaphragm in their equipment. Arctic Gas had proposed a solution to the problem of building a pipeline through permafrost by chilling the gas to below-freezing temperatures when it passed through permafrost areas. Tests showed, however, that the chilled pipe attracted moisture from soil below the pipeline. This buildup of ice then gradually causes upward pressure on the pipeline which, conceivably, could lead to cracking after several years.

The Arctic Gas plan for dealing with this frost-heave problem was to weight down the pipeline with overburden taken from along the route. When Edward Penner, a geotechnical investigator with the National Research Council borrowed Arctic Gas' equipment to duplicate the tests and measure the upward ice pressure, he discovered a leak in the diaphragm of the test equipment, which caused the tests to show much less pressure from frost heave than actually occurred. When the actual pressure from frost heave was known, Arctic Gas realized that its proposed solution would not work, and had to come up with a hastily-designed new one.

Ironically, one of the companies in the competing applicant group, Foothills Pipe Lines, had run its own tests of the Arctic Gas frost-heave solution design and had informed the National Energy Board in May 1976 that the solution designed for Arctic Gas by its Calgary consultants, Northern Engineering Services, would not work. The Foothills solution to frost-heave problems in permafrost was to wrap the pipe with polystyrofoam insulation six inches thick and then enclose it in a further insulating bed of gravel.

The new Arctic Gas frost-heave solution was enormously complex and, in its opponents' view, totally impractical. It entailed providing a system to electrically heat sections of its pipeline where insulation was thought necessary to avoid frost heave. Its plans called for establishing some 15 diesel-powered and 13 thermal electric generators along the most northerly sections of its route to provide the electricity to heat the pipeline sections. The wires feeding this electricity to the heat tracers under the pipeline would require some 300 miles of underground trenching and 400 miles of overhead power transmission lines up the Mackenzie Valley.

The Arctic Gas design, filed with the NEB in February 1977, also provided for drilling small holes and inserting electrically-powered cartridge heaters every 15 feet over a section of its pipeline from 119 to 175 miles long. This would require about 41,000 such heaters. But Foothills designers, after a review of the new Arctic Gas frost-heave design, argued before the NEB that its opponent had erred again: its mathematics had predicted twice as much frost-heave as was likely, so the proposed solution was twice what it needed to be.

Foothills also checked the Arctic Gas claim that the cartridge heaters, costing about $10 each, would last for 15 years in their holes from 30 to 65 feet deep and learned that the manufacturers said the heaters were intended to have an operating life of only about five years. Foothills also argued that to achieve what Arctic Gas expected of them, the heaters would have to operate at temperatures that would cause water in the permafrost soil to boil. If run at lower temperatures, the heaters would have to be spaced every three feet, and Arctic Gas would require 200,000 of them. In addition, the heaters would probably have to be replaced three or four times during the anticipated 20 to 25-year life of the pipeline.

The problems of having to constantly supply and service the diesel and thermal electric generators in isolated areas, of laying not only pipe but high-tension power line under such difficult sections as Shallow Bay in the Mackenzie Delta, and of maintaining 10,000 power poles along a 400-mile stretch of the Mackenzie Valley were only a few of the reasons Foothills witnesses gave before the NEB for their belief that the Arctic Gas pipeline either could not be built according to this design, or could be built only with massive overruns in estimates of costs.

Birdsong

Some of the more interesting methods of studying the Arctic ecology were developed for the birds. These began with aerial surveys to locate concentrations of large birds. Ground surveys were then carried out in areas where concentrations of birds had been spotted, and in poorly-drained areas with good potential as waterfowl habitat. A sampling method was developed intended to indicate the number of birds for each species in selected sections of the pipeline route.

Since little study had previously been done about the effect of human intrusion into wilderness bird habitats in the North, studies were developed to investigate the impact of three types of disturbances: noise from stationary sources such as compressor stations or excavating drag lines; noise from moving sources such as airplanes, helicopters or hovercraft; and noise from camp and other activities resulting from human presence. Low-flying aircraft were used, along with a machine built to simulate the sound of a pipeline compressor station, and many weeks were spent observing the effect of these noises on birds from a total of 38 sites.

These sites were chosen at intervals, so as to cover the entire route. Locations were largely determined by the availability of water bodies large enough on which to land a single-engined float-equipped airplane. Mountain areas were reached by helicopter. Four observers, working in pairs, measured the bird population at each site. Each pair walked a set of four 20-yard-wide transects, each about half a mile long and each set usually laid out in a square or rectangular pattern, the fourth ending at the beginning of the first.

All birds seen by the observers were noted on field data sheets. Each bird was identified by species when possible, and notes were made on its sex, age and behaviour. The location of each bird was recorded as "on transect" (within the 20-yard strip), or "off transect" (outside of the strip). Birds spotted flying over the transect were recorded as on transect. Many birds, however, were identified by their songs alone.

On this bird survey methodology, the Arctic Gas brief said:

> A large proportion of some species was identified by song alone, which posed the following problems: First, the observers had to be sure that a correct identification was made (errors were minimized by ensuring that an observer familiar with bird songs was present on each set of transects); Second, it was often difficult to keep track of the location of a singing bird, so often an arbitrary decision had to be made as to whether one or more birds were singing. . . .
>
> Many species were curious and therefore highly visible; others were more retiring. For example, family groups of gray jays often followed the observers along a transect course, so a high proportion of these birds were counted. Other species were shy and retiring (e.g., ovenbirds, ruby-crowned kinglets) and, although many had distinctive songs, they were rarely seen. . . . Secretive species were most detectable when song intensity was highest, but it was impossible to run all transects during the peak singing periods. Although a set of four transects can normally be run over the course of three or four hours, a levelling off of song intensity was usually noticed during the last transects.

Since food for most birds in the Arctic is available only during the short summers, the pipeline bird watchers concluded that food supply is as important to birds' migratory patterns as their biological rhythms. If their timing gets out of step with the weather, or vice versa, disaster can strike without warning from natural causes.

The snow goose, for example, must not arrive on its nesting grounds before enough vegetative forage has been exposed by the melting snows to sustain it. Yet neither must it arrive so late that it and its young born that summer cannot be fat and strong in time to wing their way south before autumn storms overtake them.

An interesting example of the importance of timing occurred during the 1972 summer field surveys. Lapland longspurs studied at the Firth and Babbage Rivers followed a precise sequence of activity. Virtually all their eggs hatched within the week of June 15 to June 22. However, when a severe and unseasonable storm hit on June 26 and did not subside until June 29, 35 per cent of the nestlings under observation died. No renesting was observed. It was assumed that although such natural disasters are not the rule, they are probably anything but rare.

The instincts which nature had bred into the king eiders can sometimes also lead to disaster. They are among the earliest migrants from western Alaska and the Bering Sea, bound for Banks Island and beyond along the Arctic coast. As many as a million birds may travel in this migration before the ice breaks up. This means that the only places for the birds to stop and feed are along the open leads or cracks in the ice which precede breakup. Some springs, when the winter lingers, the open leads do not appear, and large numbers of the king eiders perish from starvation and exposure. As such occurrences are not uncommon, the bird biologists concluded that this was nature's way of keeping the king eider population in balance.

Peregrine Falcon and Other Rare Birds

In the northern Yukon and Mackenzie Valley regions through which a pipeline may be built, a minimum of 230 species of birds, belonging to 41 bird families, have been identified as nesters, migrants or casual visitors. Several of these species may simply have been passing through, as they are not traditionally found in the project area. Many other species live all over the continent, so their survival is not at risk from routes favoured by either pipeline proposal.

The species vulnerable to the impact of a northern pipeline are those whose numbers are already low or declining, either on a continental or regional basis, or those which gather in the project area in significant numbers at some stage in their existence. For other species, a substantial part of their remaining nesting or other critical habitat lies within the proposed pipeline region.

The most important bird populations in the northern Yukon and Mackenzie Valley regions affected, from an ecological point of view, are what are known to specialists in this field as raptors, as well as certain water birds. Raptors include such rare birds as golden eagles, bald eagles, ospreys, gyrfalcons and peregrine falcons. Those in the pipeline region represent significant portions of their entire remaining North American populations. Though the golden and bald eagles are still quite numerous in other regions of the continent, as is the osprey, this rarity is especially true of the peregrine falcon and gyrfalcon. For this reason, peregrine popula-

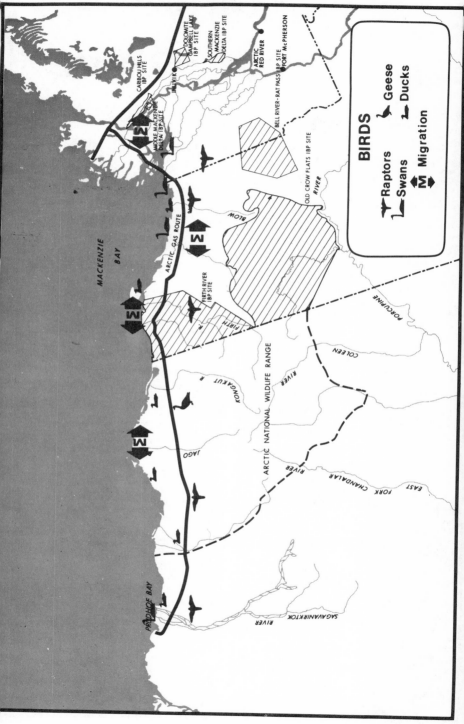

Arctic Gas Project — North Slope

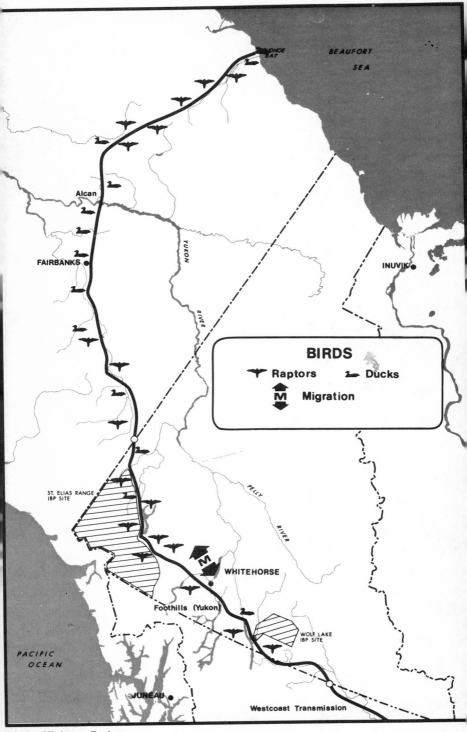

Alaska Highway Project

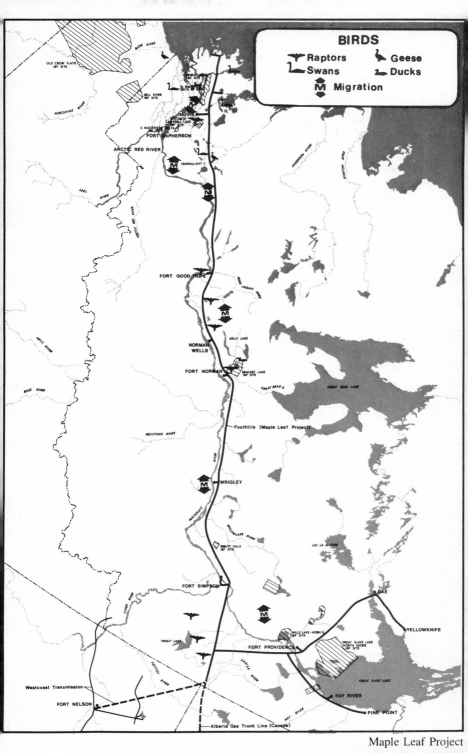

Maple Leaf Project

tions have been the most thoroughly inventoried and their critical nesting areas have also been identified in greater detail. The gyrfalcon, which does not migrate over long distances, may be present in the pipeline regions the year-round. Eagles and ospreys arrive on their annual migrations from the south as early as March and the peregrine falcon in April.

The care taken for the preservation of the peregrine falcon in the project planning of both applicant groups was offered as a specific example of the new capitalist development ethic discussed in earlier sections. Since this planning began in earnest in 1970, hundreds of hours and many thousands of dollars have been devoted simply to identifying peregrine falcon nesting sites and learning everything possible about their reproduction habits, both from existing literature and observation. The peregrine needs seclusion for successful nesting and brood raising. Intrusion by man into critical peregrine nesting areas in other regions has reduced the survivors of its species mainly to those in the north where the only adequately secluded habitat is left for its survival needs.

The only viable remaining Canadian peregrine population, with the exception of the Peale's peregrine on the Pacific coast, is found north of the 60th parallel. Fewer than 200 individual peregrines, including 77 breeding pairs, were observed in the North during 1975. Besides a loss of habitat, another factor which has contributed to the decline of the peregrine has been the accumulation of pesticide residues in their bodies which have impaired development of embryos and egg shell. The two basic concerns about the peregrine's continued survival are preservation of individual nest sites and preservation of the wilderness aspects of areas surrounding the sites.

The Berger Inquiry staff report recommended that public documents should not reveal any details about locations of peregrine nests. "Such wide knowledge," the report warned, "could lead to high losses of nestlings and eggs. Knowledge of nest locations would also lead to increased disturbance by naturalists and the general public, who, however well-intentioned, may approach eyries to observe or photograph the birds." The staff agreed with one report which pointed out that because of the great danger to the survival of peregrines, developers would have to face the fact that destruction of a single nest site or interference with nesting in a single year would have a serious and unacceptable impact — a constraint that applied to no other bird along either applicant's proposed pipeline.

A typical example of the kind of ecological studies sponsored by the applicant groups can be found in a report to Foothills Pipe Lines Limited on a biological field program conducted during the summer of 1975. It was carried out by the Lombard North Group Limited of Calgary. The purpose of the program was to complete a preliminary biological assessment of sites to be used during construction and operation of the proposed Maple Leaf line. The sites included proposed locations for compressor stations, construction camps, borrow pits from which gravel would be dug, wharves and stockpiling areas. Where any of these sites were found to encounter extreme biological sensitivity, they would be abandoned.

In the particular case of the peregrine falcon, the biologists found some cliffs along the proposed route which seemed promising as peregrine falcon nesting places. They also found other nesting places for peregrine falcons that conflicted with the pipeline route. One was so serious that a route change was proposed. This would mean finding a new site for a compressor station and a wharf. Out of such studies came recommendations, as well, for regulation of aircraft flights over ecologically-sensitive areas during specific times when this sensitivity is greatest — in the case of nesting peregrine falcons between mid-April and mid-September. During this time, it is recommended that aircraft fly at least at 1,000 feet and preferably 2,500 feet above identified nesting areas.

Ecology maps were prepared by the applicants to depict all known peregrine falcon nesting areas along the proposed routes, plus a great deal of detailed information about other birds, animals and fish at pipeline river crossings.

An environmental statement prepared for the NEB by Arctic Gas included this entry, which explained the attention given to this particular bird: "Peregrine falcon (*Falco peregrinus*) — Rare and endangered, perilously near extinction. Extirpated from all of continent, except far North, in recent years. Arctic and Subarctic regions probably contain most if not all of remaining breeding birds. Nest sites confidential; poaching danger critical."

Many volumes are now available about birds alone in the proposed project region, not to mention as many more volumes about animals and fish. Much of the information in these volumes is new, gathered painstakingly by both applicant groups. The reccommendations for the protection of raptorial birds during pipeline construction and operation by the Berger Inquiry staff typifies the unprecedented attention to ecological impact being paid by planners of this development project.

The staff report recommendations include these stringent regulations:

1. To assure incorporation of raptor concerns, especially those for peregrine falcons and gyrfalcons, the company shall consult with the Canadian Wildlife Service (CWS) raptor biologist during all planning, design, logistics, construction and operation phases of the pipeline project.

2. In all raptor protection zones identified by the government, the company shall control, restrict or otherwise alter its terrestrial and airborne activities and those of its contractors and subcontractors in such a manner as to avoid disturbance of the raptor and to conform to the directions of the CWS raptor biologist and the agency given overall authority for pipeline planning, to be decided by the federal Government.

3. All pipeline-related activities, including all forms of human access within a raptor protection zone, shall be covered by a separate construction application. The application shall be supported by documents, studies and site-specific plans that demonstrate that the proposed activity will not jeopardize the raptor nesting success in any way.

4. The company shall cease all activities within designated raptor protection zones during the sensitive periods and no later than the first day of territorial occupation by a raptor. Activities shall not recommence until the agency has provided written permission to continue the work.

5. Where project activities are permitted within a raptor protection zone during a time preceding the sensitive period, the company shall be fully prepared to cease all operations and temporarily abandon all equipment as soon as the bird takes possession of the nest site.

6. Aircraft shall maintain an altitude of at least 2,500 feet above ground level while over any raptor protection zone during the sensitive period. Lower level flights shall be diverted around the zone.

7. Airstrips and helicopter pads shall be located so that all approaches and takeoffs avoid the raptor protection zones as noted.

8. Pipeline surveillance flights less than 2,500 feet above ground level, helicopter landings and motorized terrestrial access for maintenance or repair shall be prohibited within a raptor protection zone during the sensitive period except as specifically authorized by the agency.

9. The company shall prohibit blasting within any raptor protection zone during the sensitive period except as authorized by the agency. Blasting at other times of the year may be permitted where the company demonstrates that the blasting would not damage the raptor nest site or its surroundings.

10. Barging operations and other pipeline material movement operations that infringe on any raptor protection zone during the sensitve period shall be subject to site-specific limitations imposed by the agency to limit disturbance to the raptors.

These detailed regulations were suggested under the general recommendation that the successful applicant "shall protect all birds and their habitat from adverse effects associated with the construction, operation and maintenance of the pipeline." In particular, the Berger Inquiry staff urged, "the company shall avoid disturbing raptor sites and important areas for waterfowl migration, nesting, feeding, moulting and staging. The government," the staff report said, "should identify important and restricted ornithological areas and periods, particularly for raptors and waterfowl such as geese, and develop and impose special restrictions on access and aircraft activities in such areas."

Waterfowl

The Mackenzie Valley is an important migration route for many birds that breed in the western Arctic and sub-Arctic every summer. During May and early June, the only available open water for large numbers of northward-bound waterfowl is among the Mackenzie River islands, from Camsell Bend to the Delta, and some of the lakes adjacent to the river. These waters are heavily used for resting, feeding and mating. As many as 200,000 geese and swans may pause on the sandbars, spits and island fringes on their northern flights. These same areas provide resting stages during the fall migration south for young birds in years when, for some reason, they do not have the energy reserves to make the long flight without interruption.

Large numbers of ducks, some Canada geese, sandhill cranes, loons, and shorebirds nest in the boreal forest and forest-tundra habitats of the Mackenzie Valley. The Berger staff concluded that the Ramparts River, Mackay Creek, Great Bear-Loche River, Mills Lake and Beaver Lake areas are the most important nesting, brood rearing, moulting and staging areas of water-oriented birds in the Mackenzie Valley between Great Slave Lake and the Delta.

On this, the staff report said:

> The Mackenzie Delta itself is one of the most important waterfowl production areas of North America, with breeding populations of several hundred thousand ducks and geese. Of particular concern are the snow goose colony at Kendall Island, with 1,200 to 8,000 breeding birds, the approximately 20,000 nesting whistling swans in the Eskimo Lakes-Liverpool Bay area, and the scarce trumpeter swan which has recently been reported nesting near Moose Channel. The uncommon Hudsonian godwit does nest in portions of the Delta and the almost-extinct Eskimo curlew may still nest on the tundra east of the project area. Many other parts of the Delta are critical for moulting ducks and geese during summer.

Second only to the Delta as a critical waterfowl production area in northwest Canada are the Old Crow Flats in the Northern Yukon interior. The Beaufort Sea coast is also important for nesting whistling swans. Brant and many other species of ducks, loons, gulls, terns and shorebirds use the coastal lagoons, beaches and islands as resting places, for nesting and later moulting areas. From June through August, the tundra lakes of the Yukon coastal plain area are important nesting, feeding, brood-rearing and moulting areas for a number of species of swan, geese, ducks, loons and shorebirds.

The tundra area near the Firth and Babbage Rivers may also be the centre of the nesting range of the uncommon buff-breasted sandpiper. The best-known rare or endangered species in northern Canada is the whooping crane, followed closely by the peregrine falcon and the golden eagle, but the Hudson godwit, Eskimo curlew and buff-breasted sandpiper are also in danger of disappearing for the same reason: disappearance of previously abundant, suitable habitat. This circumstance in southern regions had left their present remnant populations concentrated in the North.

In the late summer and autumn as many as 300,000 to 500,000 geese, swans and ducks gather on the Yukon coastal plain and the Shallow Bay coastal area for a period of concentrated feeding to build up the energy reserves needed for the long flight south. The major waterfowl present during this period are the snow goose (whose nesting can be disturbed, pipeline ecology studies have shown, by aircraft flying over as high as 10,000 feet above ground level). On any given day in August, almost the entire western Arctic waterfowl population might be gathered on the coastal plain, between Bathurst Peninsula and the Canning River in Alaska.

Obviously, any pipeline activity that would mean serious damage to wetlands in these regions, either by causing them to drain or flood, would greatly harm waterfowl habitat. The pipeline poses similar problems to fish in the region.

Fish

Two types of fish are found in most of the flowing water systems and lakes in the regions of the proposed pipeline routes, those that spawn in the spring and those that spawn in the fall. Spring spawners are less of a concern for pipeliners than fall spawners. The spring spawners deposit their eggs at the breakup of winter ice and the young emerge within a few weeks. The eggs of the fall spawners, however, have to survive the rigours of a northern winter, lying in the gravel from October until breakup the following May or June, when the fry hatch and move to their nursery areas.

Arctic fish grow slowly, are often large for their species, and are late to mature sexually. As a result, there is usually a large stock in most areas, but productivity is low. If anything happened to reduce the standing stock, it would be slow to replenish. Some Northern fish spend their lives entirely in freshwater, others in saltwater, and others move between the two. Some Arctic char, for example, live only in freshwater. Others of the same species migrate to sea. Many whitefish and lake trout also use productive lakes as substitutes for the sea throughout much of the Arctic. Most Northern fish have specific migration routes, and limited spawning, overwintering, nursery and feeding areas — another basic consideration for pipeliners in the North.

Because it originates in a southern climate less severe than that of the Arctic, the Mackenzie River is more productive of fish and the food to support them than rivers from either the Porcupine or North Slope drainages of the northwestern Arctic. Thirty-four species have been found in the Mackenzie River, sixteen in rivers

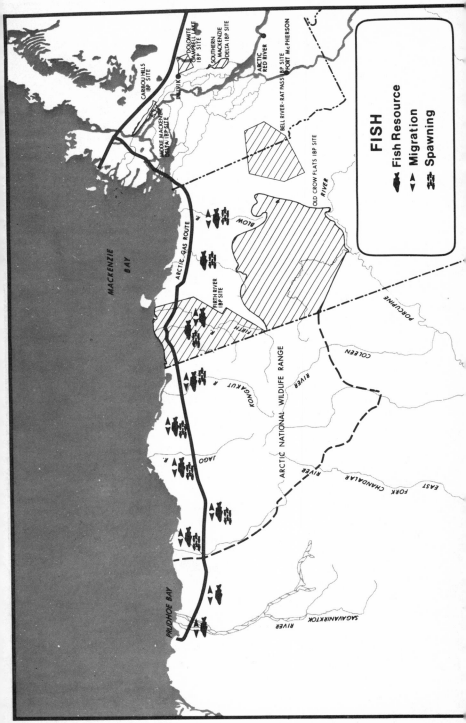

Arctic Gas Project — North Slope

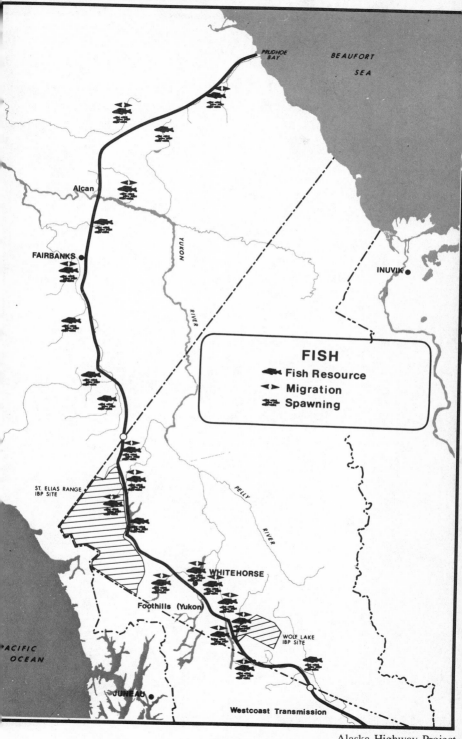

FISH

Fish Resource
Migration
Spawning

Alaska Highway Project

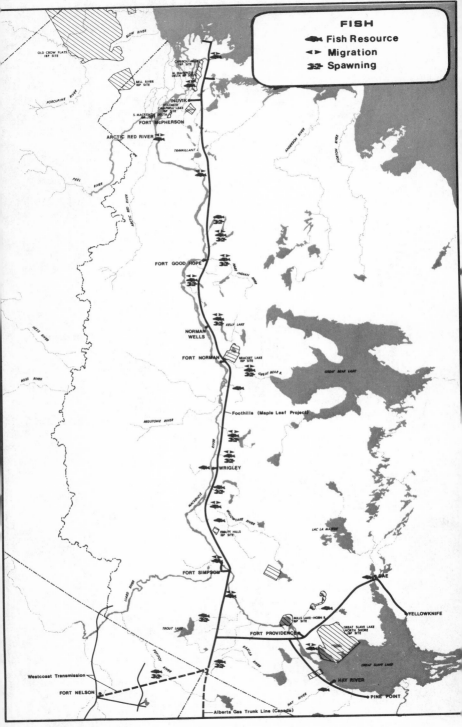

Maple Leaf Project

from the Porcupine, and seven in Yukon North Slope rivers. Significant runs of Pacific salmon occur in the Porcupine-Yukon rivers, and Arctic char are present in the North Slope and Delta rivers, but few salmon or char are found in the Mackenzie River south of the Delta.

Sixty-two per cent of the species in the Mackenzie River are fall spawners and 35 per cent spring spawners. A variety of species in the whitefish family dominate the fall spawners in the Mackenzie. They begin migrating through the Delta waters in August and spawn in the upper Delta, Arctic Red, Peel and Mackenzie mainstem rivers in September and early October. After spawning, whitefish runs occur back down these rivers in late October and November.

The fishery along the proposed pipeline routes has three uses: for sport, commercial and domestic use. The most important use is as a local source of protein. Fish have traditionally been an important part of the diet in northern communities, both for the human inhabitants and the sled dogs. The domestic fishery has declined as dogteams have been replaced by the snowmobile, but the annual catch is still very important to Northern people.

The greatest source of potential damage from pipelining would be siltation that might alter fish habitat, smother fish eggs, or displace spawning grounds. These effects could be caused by digging trenches for pipeline river crossings or by removing gravel to build pads or berms on top of the permafrost. In order to avoid this sort of damage, the applicant groups have done extensive studies to locate spawning grounds along their proposed routes, so that they can either alter the routes or plan construction for times when there would be the least risk to the spawning fish or their eggs.

Other dangers which their studies warned them of include changing water temperature and levels of dissolved oxygen in the water, or causing other chemical changes in water that would be harmful to fish, including spills of toxic materials.

Mammals

There seems to be little reason to worry about the impact of a pipeline on the survival of smaller animals along the proposed routes, whether they live (like shrews, lemmings, mice, squirrels and moles) on the ground or (like muskrat and beaver) in the water, because they have such a rapid reproduction capacity.

For the larger animals, however, there is a basic concern about maintaining their traditional habitat quality. There is also concern to prevent over-hunting, disturbances which may interfere with breeding or remaining in their familiar habitat, and creation of physical barriers such as snow fences, unburied pipe and long open trenches that may interfere with migratory patterns.

Caribou and Reindeer

The possible interference with migratory patterns of caribou and reindeer was a special concern in determining the potential impact of a pipeline. The Arctic Gas route across the northern Yukon would cut through the range of the Porcupine caribou herd so valued by the Indians of Old Crow. Either the Arctic Gas or Maple Leaf route up the Mackenzie would pass through the reindeer grazing preserve and skirt the range of the Bluenose caribou herd. Other petroleum industry activities, such as drilling and operating gas wells, feeder pipelines, and processing plants would also affect caribou and reindeer in these regions.

The studies of caribou and reindeer migratory patterns would be used to schedule construction of a pipeline at times that would not interfere with migration, calving or nursing of young. The pipeline would be designed so that it would not create obstructions to migration. Aircraft flights over caribou herds at sensitive times would also be restricted to a minimum altitude of 2,500 feet for adequate protection of herds during sensitive times in their life-cycle. Aircraft movements over occupied caribou range in winter would be confined to flight corridors corresponding, wherever possible, to the pipeline right-of-way or access roads.

Other Animals

Similar studies and plans for protection have been carried out on grizzly, polar and black bears, moose, Dall sheep, and Arctic and coloured foxes. Moose and bear are the most likely to be troubled by pipelining. Dall sheep and foxes face little risk.

Moose have been known to panic when aircraft fly low over them; helicopters in particular upset them. With bears, the problems are not unlike the problems which man has with bears in the south. They are attracted by food and garbage, so special plans have been made to keep garbage and food not only out of their reach at pipeline camps, but in containers intended to minimize

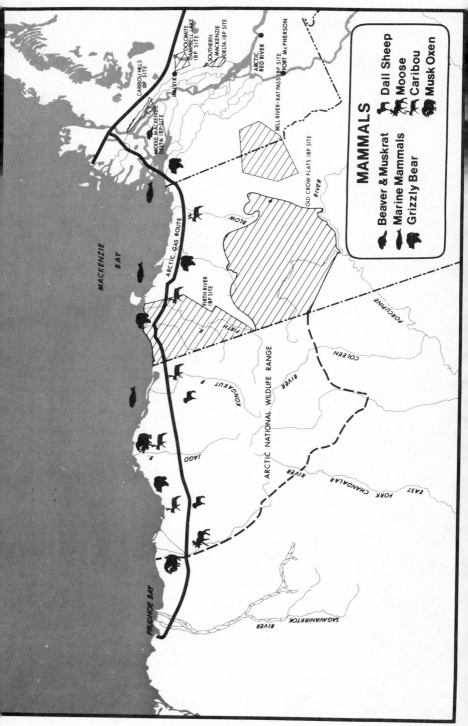

Arctic Gas Project — North Slope

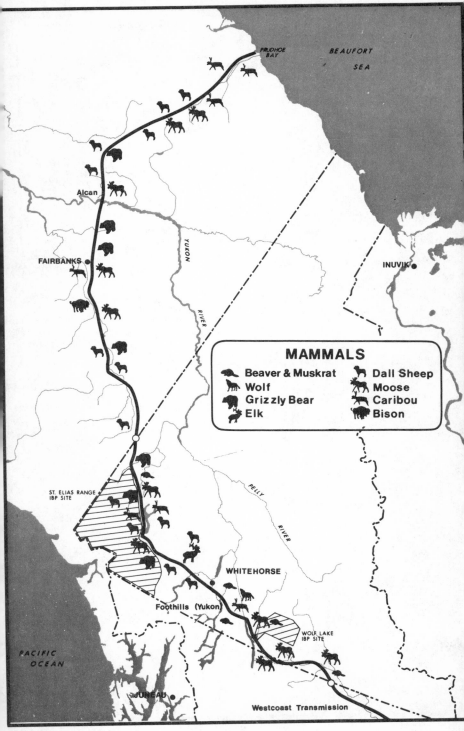

MAMMALS

- Beaver & Muskrat
- Wolf
- Grizzly Bear
- Elk
- Dall Sheep
- Moose
- Caribou
- Bison

PRUDHOE BAY

BEAUFORT SEA

Alcan

FAIRBANKS

INUVIK

YUKON

RIVER

ST. ELIAS RANGE IBP SITE

PELLY RIVER

WHITEHORSE

Foothills (Yukon)

WOLF LAKE IBP SITE

PACIFIC OCEAN

JUNEAU

Westcoast Transmission

Alaska Highway Project

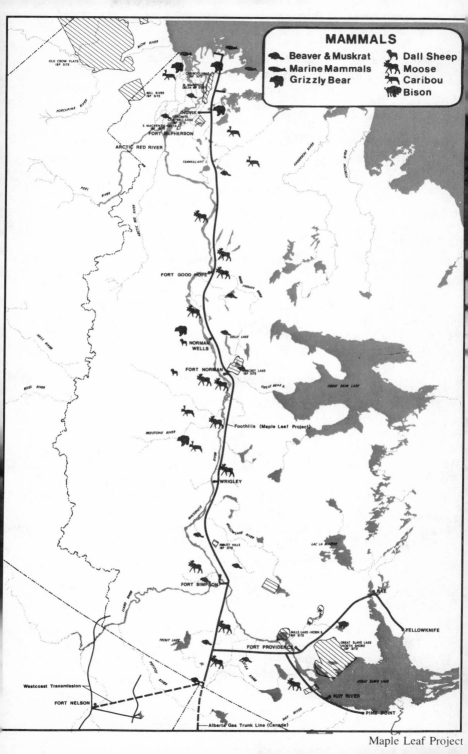

Maple Leaf Project

attracting smells until burned in high-temperature incinerators. However, the critical element for the bears is that their winter denning sites not be disturbed. The Berger Inquiry staff report stressed that:

> Any activity which results in the winter disturbance and abandonment of a den may lead to the death from exposure of the affected bear. Harassment, especially from airplanes, can also be very detrimental. Bears can expend vast amounts of energy trying to evade the airborne intruder. This loss of stored energy may be crucial to the bear's survival over the winter.

White Whales

The route preferred by Arctic Gas across the Delta would pose a threat to the white, or beluga, whales which use the Mackenzie estuary, particularly Mackenzie, Shallow and Shoalwater Bays, as nursing and rearing areas. Upwards of 4,000 white whales use these waters from June to August. Their time of arrival depends on ice conditions. The shallow, relatively warm waters and the plentiful food sources provide ideal habitat for the cow whales with young calves. The potential for disturbing these marine mammals was summarized in the Berger Inquiry staff report:

> Large amounts of supplies and equipment for construction in the Delta area will be moved through the Mackenzie Bay from Alaska and brought down the Mackenzie River on ships and barges. The disturbance of whales, in the west Mackenzie Bar area, from this increased water-based transport during the summer, could result from the increased noise and possible oil or chemical spills from these vessels. Summer construction of the proposed cross-Delta pipeline may cause further harassment of the white whales. Installation of the pipeline, underwater blasting, the presence of barges, air cushion and other construction-related transportation vehicles in the area, could disturb nursing whales. Air cushion vehicles are especially disturbing to white whales. Noise usually frightens the whales into deeper water, thereby affecting calves which need shallow, warm water for surface breathing and maintenance of body heat.

The report recommended that the government designate a whale sanctuary in Mackenzie and Shallow Bays. This would exclude development activity in that area used by calving and nursing whales. The report also recommended that the pipeline be rerouted south of the area used by the whales. If this were not done, then that section of the pipeline should only be built when the whales were not present in the area.

7

PEOPLE PROBLEMS

Never in the history of Canada has there been a royal commission quite like the Mackenzie Valley Pipeline Inquiry. In all the points the news media have made about the inquiry, this one seems to have been missed. The news media representatives covering the inquiry concentrated, rightly, on the social, environmental, ecological and economic issues raised for assessment, in connection with pipeline plans, during the 20 months of hearings; but these issues were neither new nor unknown. What was unique about the inquiry was the inquiry itself. Never before had such an intensive study been made of such issues prior to a development project.

The inquiry, headed by Mr. Justice Thomas Rodney Berger of the British Columbia Supreme Court, spent a total of 302 days listening to evidence from 1,000 witnesses during hearings at 35 Northern communities and settlements throughout the Mackenzie region. Sometimes the hearings were convened in tiny meeting halls, and occasionally in the open beside a river; the modes of travel used by the commission included dogsled and canoe. Hearings were also held in 11 cities in southern Canada from coast to coast. Transcripts of the testimony filled 277 volumes — more than 50,000 pages and an estimated 14 million words. In addition, many thousands of pages of prepared evidence were also filed. Berger said that the inquiry would finally cost $4.5 million, including $1.5 million that went to fund native and other public interest groups. The commission took this step to ensure that opponents of the pipeline could face the petroleum industry on a more equal footing.

And for whom? For what amounts to a miniscule proportion of the Canadian population — in all about 38,000 souls: some 7,500 Indians, possibly close to 14,000 Inuit (Eskimos), about 10,000 Metis, and the rest, about 6,800, whites. Add to the information about the needs and aspirations of these people that the Berger Inquiry has collected what the competing applicants have learned about them, and what has been presented during hearings in the region by the National Energy Board — and beyond doubt, the people of the Mackenzie must be the most thoroughly analyzed and profoundly examined minority group in any population on earth.

(A mini-Berger Inquiry to study the social and economic impact of the proposed Alaska Highway pipeline was announced in April 1977 by Northern Affairs Minister Warren Allmand; Kenneth Lysyk, former deputy attorney general of Saskatchewan and then dean of law at the University of British Columbia, was appointed chairman and assigned to complete the studies between May 1 and August 1. The environmental aspects of the proposed Alaska Highway line were assigned for review to a panel of the federal Environment Department, headed by V. M. Hill, vice-chairman of the office responsible for the department's assessment and review process. Allmand said in his news announcement that if the Alaska line were approved, Ottawa would establish a further inquiry to help develop terms and conditions for construction and operation of the line.)

The existence of the Berger Inquiry, whatever it might finally claim to have accomplished, was in itself the best evidence that capitalist development ethics must change. However, the precedent of taking the human element into account in all manner of development projects was not established by the Berger Inquiry. The inquiry only confirmed a policy already in an advanced stage of evolution. And we should be clear what is meant by ''the human element.'' The term encompasses both ecological and environmental considerations, along with socio-economic evaluations; but all of these considerations, finally, have their most important impact on people.

The change in the capitalist development ethic represented by the Berger Inquiry was a shift in emphasis away from giving economic benefit the major, even the sole, priority in assessing a project's worth. People, the environment and ecology have become nearly as important as profit.

The first major stage to appear in the evolution of this new approach to development was in Alaska, where it was evoked by the debate over the Alyeska oil pipeline. The record showed that the human element was a fundamental part of the initial concepts for an Arctic natural gas pipeline developed by the Alberta Gas Trunk Line in the spring of 1970, several months before the Canadian government's first northern pipeline guidelines.

The government guidelines ensured that people would have to be given serious consideration in any pipeline project finally approved in the Mackenzie region. The effect of the Berger Inquiry on the political climate, not only in the Mackenzie region but in all of Canada may, hopefully, ensure that people will not be forgotten in future development projects. However, at this stage, it is no more than a hope. The extent to which the needs of people are cared for in the construction of whatever gas pipeline finally is built south from the Arctic will strengthen that hope.

The Berger Inquiry began and ended with no consensus about any gas pipeline up the Mackenzie Valley. It may have been thought at the outset that the inquiry would be concerned mainly about the potential impact of a pipeline on the fragile ecosystems of the region or the raw but delicate elements of an environment still largely undisturbed by the activities of modern man. Instead, the concerns of the people living in the region rapidly came to the fore in the hearings.

Consequently, it may be argued, the Berger Inquiry produced a singular political issue. Within the Mackenzie region itself, the inquiry discovered that some of the Northerners who were living there wanted the pipeline for its economic benefits, while others opposed it for fear of how it would affect their way of life. No decision about a pipeline would please everyone, even within the relatively tiny population involved in the Mackenzie region itself. So whose interests should be served in the region?

The larger political issue concerns the interests of the rest of the Canadian population, not to mention the interests of Canada's best neighbours, the Americans. Can, or should, the interests of what in fact is only a fraction of a fraction of the Canadian people be given priority over the interests of the majority? Or is there possible ground for a compromise that might not satisfy anyone completely, yet may be seen to be as fair and just as any reasonable person should expect?

Native Land Claims

The search for an answer will probably be aided by establishing what land claims the native peoples in the Mackenzie region are making, and who these native peoples are. It is estimated, by the Berger Inquiry staff, that the native population of about 16,000 in the main impact region of the pipeline consists of the following components:

1. About 7,500 treaty Indians, all living around Great Slave Lake, along the Mackenzie River system and in the Delta.
2. About 4,500 Metis (part-Indian), most of whom live around Great Slave Lake and in the Delta.
3. Some 3,500 Inuit, all living north of the Arctic Circle.

These figures do not include perhaps another 500 native people living in communities some distance away from the proposed pipeline route up the valley. The total native population significantly outnumbers the non-native population in the region, which is estimated at about 10,000. Even within this regional population, there are opposite views about the pipeline.

There is also considerable dissension within the ranks of the native people's groups putting the land claims forward.

Early in 1976, the Inuit Tapirisat of Canada, representing the major (Eskimo) territorial racial bloc, laid claim to large areas of land and water in the western Arctic above the treeline. Their claim for a Nunavit territory proposed that their aboriginal rights to 700,000 square miles of land and 800,000 square miles of ocean be relinquished, in return for title to 250,000 square miles of land including subsurface rights down to 1,500 feet. The land would be held in communal form by the community and regional corporations to be established under the terms of the proposal.

A central feature of the proposal was that Inuit be allowed to select 50,000 square miles of the 250,000, in which any existing rights, such as oil and gas leases, held by outsiders could be cancelled, subject to compensation being paid by the federal government to the rights holder. Inuit land could then be expropriated only by a special act of Parliament, not existing laws. In other words, no development of Inuit lands could take place without Inuit consent, unless Parliament itself intervened.

163

Before the end of the year, however, the Tapirisat had to withdraw this land claim while further consultation was carried out among the widely-scattered members of the organization. Then just before Christmas, the Committee for Original People's Entitlement (COPE), representing Inuit in the key Beaufort Sea area, decided to go ahead with a regional land claim of its own. In March 1977 these claims were neither in final shape nor obviously close to settlement.

The most controversial land claim came from the Northwest Territories Indian Brotherhood, headed by former telephone line repairman George Erasmus. The brotherhood claims to represent the Dene, a native word meaning nation or the people, of the Northwest Territories. At one point, the brotherhood was supported by the Metis Association, but during a period of some confusion over the brotherhood's intentions, when it seemed to be demanding that a Mackenzie native people's separate state be approved by Ottawa, the Metis broke away.

The Dene claim, as a negotiating position, ownership, through aboriginal title, of 450,000 square miles of land within the Territories, mainly in the Mackenzie Valley region. Since bones of their ancestors and artifacts found in the region prove that there were Dene living along the Great Slave and Great Bear Lakes and the Mackenzie River before Rome was built, the Dene argue that they are only asking for recognition of their right to their traditional homeland. The Dene took their case for a legal right to freeze land transactions throughout much of the Mackenzie Valley all the way to the Supreme Court of Canada, but in December 1976 the court ruled 9 to 0 against their claim to this power.

The Dene declared before the Berger Inquiry that they were poor and dependent on the whites because Ottawa had wrongfully taken control of the wealth under their lands, wealth which would have given the Dene income to pay their own way. They also seemed to be asking for the land which they claim to be treated as a sort of reserve, over which they would exercise their own rule.

Appearing before the National Energy Board in March 1977, Erasmus continued his campaign opposing any pipeline being laid in the Mackenzie Valley for at least 10 to 15 years, and certainly not before the land claims were settled. Under lengthy cross-examination, he conceded that since 1970 there have been some gradual changes in the education system in the North, in favour of more teaching of native languages, and with greater awareness of distinctive native cultural interests. But he was insistent that these changes were too slow and too little. He said:

> This is what we seek: to be able to develop an economy which would be self-contained, as much as possible. There would be interaction of all kinds, but the things that would be important would be the kinds of control mechanisms that the Dene themselves would have over their own economy. And we have to have some kind of political control, so that the area that we are living in we have some control of.

Erasmus stated that the Dene needed time to build up cultural resistance to the impact of such a huge development as a pipeline. At another point he said that the Dene wanted to set up relatively self-contained communities similar to the Hutterite colonies in southern Canada. "What we are talking about when I say survive is mainly our culture" he said, and maintained that this depended heavily on restoring the native language to the Dene school system. One thing Dene history had taught since contact with white civilization was that:

> . . . as younger Dene people lose their language . . . the values of the other cultures are introduced quicker and quicker. . . . The language itself, in its mannerisms and in its approach to interpreting life, carries all kinds of values. . . . If it could be maintained, you would be able to preserve an incredible amount of your culture.

The Metis Association announced its break with the Indian Brotherhood as the Berger Inquiry was wrapping up its hearings in Yellowknife in November 1976. The president, Rick Hardy, told Berger that the land claims should be settled before a pipeline was built. He also said that the Metis saw their future depending upon Northern development, and the pipeline was the most immediate opportunity to stimulate this development. The land no longer sustained northern peoples. There was a need for economic growth and the new jobs that come with it.

In the Yukon, the Council for Yukon Indians also laid claim to land rights in proposed pipeline corridors, on behalf of the native people of Old Crow. This ancient village depended for centuries on the game in the area, in particular the caribou that move annually by the thousands across Old Crow Flats. Evidence was presented to the inquiry that the Kutchin Indians of Old Crow had maintained a caribou hunting camp at Klokut, on the Porcupine River, for at least 1,000 years. Evidence had also been found at the same site of aboriginal men dating back to 27,000 years ago.

The Berger Inquiry staff summed up the native peoples' land claims this way:

> The land claims of the Dene and the Inuit are premised on a claim to self-determination; the land claims are seen as a major break from the settlements which have been made with the native people in the past. They seek a guarantee of the right to the cultural survival and integrity of native people of the North through a new Confederation in accordance with the spirit of 1867. The people of the Mackenzie Valley, Mackenzie Delta and the northern Yukon have clearly placed their hopes in the land claims to fulfill their vision for the future. The settlement of the land claims is therefore a real and symbolic event in their relationship to the rest of Canada.

The staff report observed that the native spokesmen left no doubt about their image of the white man's government: "In the eyes of the native people, we have abused their land and resources, we have ignored and trampled on their traditions, we have increasingly circumscribed their right to control their own lives." The pipeline thus had become "a real and symbolic event" measuring the relationship between the white and native worlds. "If a decision is made to build the pipeline prior to the settlement of land claims, it will be a clear demonstration to them that the Government is not prepared to give them the right to govern their own lives."

The staff report also took note of the positions of the applicant groups on native land claims. The Foothills group, through Bob Blair, said that it believed the land claims should be settled before a pipeline was built in the Mackenzie Valley. Blair reiterated that the Maple Leaf pipeline proposal, not being dependent in any way on the urgent need of moving Alaskan gas to the lower United States, allowed for time to settle the claims. The Arctic Gas group, through Arctic Gas president Vern Horte, accepted the importance of settling the land claims, but took the view that the land claims were a separate issue and that construction could start on the Arctic Gas pipeline prior to settlement of the claims, and Arctic Gas would be prepared to do so.

James Bay Settlement

Native organizations referred to the native peoples' land claims settlement against the James Bay hydro-power project in Northern Quebec. This settlement was negotiated while the project was under construction. The native spokesmen compared it, in Berger Inquiry appearances, to negotiating with a gun at their heads. The Crees of James Bay, however, in their evidence to Berger in Montreal, denied this; they said that their settlement had been freely negotiated and agreed. Summarizing this evidence, the staff report said that the Crees testified that the James Bay settlement "has had the result of putting the Cree people into an independent position not only to face the Government of Quebec and the Government of Canada, but also to face the society in which they have to participate, not as spectators but as participants and decision-makers of the future — a future decided by the Cree themselves." The agreement would preserve their culture and society.

"Now if these be the results of the agreement," commented the staff report, "they are not that different from those which we understand to be the objectives of the Dene and the Inuit in their land claims."

Under the James Bay agreement, the Cree and the Inuit of the James Bay region surrendered their aboriginal rights in return for specific interests in three categories of land:

1. Lands allocated to the native peoples for their exclusive use; these were lands in and around the communities where they normally live and roughly correspond to Indian reserve lands. Except for existing rights and public use such as roads and easements for utilities, no development can take place on these lands without the consent of the native people. They comprise about 3,250 square miles for the Inuit and 2,158 square miles for the Crees.

(These lands and the native peoples' rights in them compare roughly to wider rights over 250,000 square miles in the western Arctic demanded by the Tapirisat Nunavit proposal and over the 450,000 square miles demanded by the Dene.)

2. Lands over which the native peoples have exclusive hunting, fishing and trapping rights, but not special rights of occupancy: 25,000 square miles designated for the Crees and 35,000 for the Inuit. Developed land in this area must be replaced or

paid for, but mineral exploration may not be charged for.

3. Public lands of the province of Quebec over which native people have the right to hunt, fish and trap and in which certain species of animals and birds are reserved for their exclusive use. Development without compensation is possible and anyone has access and use.

The agreement also provided for a monetary settlement amounting to $225 million to be paid over a 20-year period. The lands are administered by committees on which native peoples, on one side, and the provincial and federal governments, on the other, have equal representation. These committees are mostly advisory, however; the ultimate power of decision lies with the Quebec government. Provision is made for setting up regional and local government institutions for Cree and Inuit, and for creation of a Cree and Inuit school board. The regional government can exert wide powers over local administration, transport, communications, justice, health and social services, education, economic development and environment, resources and land-use management — all areas in which the Inuit and Dene in the Mackenzie region seek control.

A drawback of the James Bay agreement, as far as Mackenzie region Inuit and the Dene are concerned, is that it was based on a decision to open the area for development. It did not provide the kind of self-determination control over their land use that the Mackenzie Inuit and Dene were demanding as part of their land settlements.

Alaska Settlement
There is an interesting difference between the provisions of the Alaska Native Claims Settlement Act and the provisions of the James Bay settlement or the demands of the Mackenzie native peoples. In a sense, it symbolizes the fundamental difference between the Canadian idea of a nation designed for unity in diversity and the American idea of unity in uniformity. Although the Alaska settlement, granting 40 million acres and $1 billion dollars to its native peoples, was a major change from previous U.S. native settlements, there was no special recognition of the native subsistence economy in the form of hunting, fishing or trapping rights, nor were any native political structures estab-

lished. In fact, any permanent racially-defined institutions, rights or obligations were specifically prohibited.

As interpreted by the Berger Inquiry staff, "the clear purpose of the [Alaska] settlement is to integrate the natives into the dominant society," whereas the settlements proposed by the Inuit and Dene in Canada's Mackenzie region "seek the preservation, not assimilation, of native culture and society."

Training Programs

Northerners, by all accounts, remain as divided in their evaluation of the Berger Inquiry as of the pipeline. Some feel that the inquiry, and visits from pipeliners before the inquiry began, only stirred up racial feeling and a variety of expectations that were bound to be disappointed, instead of solving anything. If this is so, Alberta Gas Trunk Line deserves a substantial share of the initial responsibility: it was first into the region with delegations of executives who tried to explain its original pipeline proposals, and with a plan for training Northerners in the skills which they might later employ on the Arctic pipeline.

The Northern training program was developed in 1970 by Alberta Gas Trunk Line. The program was a part of the original concept, a commitment to employ as many Northerners as possible in both the construction and operation of the proposed pipeline project.

If Northerners (Indian, Inuit, Metis, or white people who have been resident for four years or longer in the North) were to enjoy employment opportunities from the pipeline, however, they would first need a chance to acquire the necessary skills. With this in view, Trunk Line conceived a program concentrating on an on-the-job training approach. It was designed not only to enable Northerners to acquire new skills and upgrade existing ones, it also offered a chance to pursue careers leading to supervisory and managerial responsibilities.

Training programs were nothing new for Northerners. They had been offered in a variety of areas by government and private industry. A general failing of previous programs had been that a trainee, having completed a course, returned North to find that no jobs were available in his newly-acquired skill. Trunk Line decided that all trainees in its new program would be hired as regular employees. They would then be given the option of remaining on staff in Alberta when their training was completed, or going back north to work on the Arctic pipeline if it was approved.

Trunk Line considered that the most important factor in the program would be the assignment of an experienced Northerner as a supervisor of the training regime — someone who could draw from personal experience to help the trainees adapt from the unstructured life of the North to the nine-to-five work-a-day routine of an operating pipeline system in the south. The man selected for this job, late in 1970, was Art Giroux of Fort Simpson, N.W.T., a former officer with the Northwest Territories industry department. Trunk Line facilities at Rocky Mountain House, in the foothills region of west-central Alberta, were chosen as the training site, because their relatively isolated surroundings are mindful of some Northern regions. Many of the trainees later agreed that the Rocky Mountain House area was a lot like home.

Giroux began recruiting for the program in late 1970. Visits to Northern communities earlier in the autumn by Trunk Line executives had included information about the program. They had found that job opportunities were a frequent preoccupation of the Northerners whom they met, whether native or white. New expectations about the future were first ignited in Northerners by these visits. Some of these expectations survived, as indicated by Berger Inquiry testimony; others have been dashed by the long wait for their realization, or turned toward political objectives such as those represented by the land claims.

Initially 16 Northerners (4 Indian, 4 Metis, 3 Inuit and 5 white) were recruited. They came from 11 communities in the Northwest Territories and the Yukon, as widely separated as Bathurst Inlet, Tuktoyaktuk, Old Crow, Whitehorse, Hay River and points in between. Early in January 1971, they moved into mobile homes set up in the local trailer park at Rocky Mountain House. Families moved into individual units of up to four bedrooms, depending on family size, while four single men shared four-bedroom trailers, all at nominal rents. The trainees were selected in co-operation with representatives of the N.W.T. government and Canada Manpower in the Yukon.

Another key element of the program was the trainee's freedom to select his preferred line of work. The orientation program which the first group was given included medical examinations, driver and first-aid training, and instruction on safety equipment and procedures. Then they were introduced to the work of gas measurement, compressor and pipeline operations — the three pipeline operation skills areas in which they could choose to be trained. After three months, the trainees went to work on other Trunk Line facilities in various parts of Alberta.

Within three months, several were capable of working on the operation of compressor stations. By the fall of 1971, one of the trainees had gained the ability and confidence to tutor newcomers as compressor station operators. Others had mastered elementary operations of meter and compressor stations, and gone on to apprentice as mechanics, instrument mechanics and millwrights under the Alberta apprenticeship board. Still others planned to apprentice in electrical skills and welding; they faced four years of training, including several months of classroom instruction, to obtain journeyman certificates. The Northerners were gradually provided the same opportunities as other Trunk Line employees to move into technical apprenticeship programs.

This training program proved successful enough to be adopted by the Northwest group when the Trunk North group joined it in 1972. The training program gradually developed into a separate entity known as Nortran (Northern Petroleum Industry Training Program), supported by both competing applicant groups. At the time that the integrated groups evolved in 1973 into the Canadian Arctic Gas Study Group, 13 of the original trainees were still with Trunk Line. Total attrition over the three and a half years had been 44 per cent.

By December 1976, seven companies were participating in the program, which offered about 107 on-the-job training positions for Northerners (20 Indian, 43 Metis, 35 Inuit and 9 white). The 1975 attrition rate was about 35 per cent. (Loneliness was their major problem in the south.) The other companies participating in Nortran, in addition to Trunk Line, were Foothills Pipe Line, Imperial Oil, Shell Canada, Gulf Oil Canada, TransCanada PipeLines, and Canadian Arctic Gas Pipeline.

Northern Development

The Arctic Gas group made a point in its socio-economic statement to the National Energy Board which is often overlooked when circumstances of native peoples in the North are being reviewed. Anyone who followed news coverage of the Berger Inquiry knows that the lifestyle of native peoples in the region through which the proposed pipeline would pass has been characterized by self-

171

sufficiency, self-determination and a deep affinity with the land, which has provided warmth, food and security for centuries. This point was hammered home endlessly in news coverage of Berger's inquiries.

The point which is hardly ever mentioned, but worth noting in the Arctic Gas brief, is this: "This style of life and means of support is part of the past of all mankind, but for the native people in the region that is being reviewed, the change from that pattern is relatively new." One of the little-emphasized issues underlying the entire Berger Inquiry was whether the old way of native life in the North was already too far in the past for retrieval. There was evidence from the native people themselves that this might be so.

Material already quoted from the Berger Inquiry staff report explained why native peoples in the Mackenzie region of the proposed pipeline found it hard to believe that there would be any lasting economic benefits for them in the project. From the days of the whalers and fur traders down to their present experiences with seismic crews, the Northerners have seen the southern entre-preneurs bring them nothing but boom and bust — with the em-phasis usually on the bust.

Despite such past disappointments, there was every reason to believe that in the case of a pipeline, this experience would be different. The federal government guidelines, plus the political climate created by the Berger Inquiry and report, should ensure that there would be lasting economic benefits in areas near a Northern pipeline, even if the extensive planning to ensure this by both applicant groups should somehow fail.

Richard Hardy, the president of the Northwest Territories Metis Association, was not the only one to express concern before the Berger Inquiry about the risks inherent in romanticizing the an-cient native tradition in the North, instead of facing the reality of current circumstances. In a 19 November 1976 appearance, Hardy said that the "Metis people object strenuously" to suggestions that an idealized way of native life, devoted exclusively to an existence based on hunting and trapping, should be dominant. "Life on the land is tough," Hardy said. "So tough that the majority of native people have left such life on the land to live in communities and have taken and accepted such things, services and commodities as government-built houses, fuel oil stoves for their heat, electricity, and food from the stores."

172

For any region to prosper requires economic development, Hardy argued:

> We cannot now endorse or suggest an economic future which will in any way hinder or adversely affect such an economic state. We therefore look to the construction of the pipeline as one of the major economic projects which we wish to take part in. . . . If we as Metis people are to survive and continue to grow socially and culturally, we must first be economically and otherwise secure. Metis people in communities and in large centres have come to depend on wages and small businesses for a living and look to that way of life in the future.

A few excerpts from the Berger Inquiry transcript, during two days in June 1975 when it visited the isolated communities of Brackett Lake and Fort Norman, revealed the conflict of past and present realities within the native communities themselves.

One witness opposed to a pipeline was youthful Chief Paul Andrew, then only 25 years old, of the Fort Norman Slavey band. He spoke of the crime rate in white southern society, of poverty, struggles for wealth and power. What, he wondered, is so civilized about this type of society referred to as the "developed country"? Then he said:

> In the Northwest Territories, we do not want to change our way of life. . . . We do not know enough of any other way of life. We can not go into the white man's world and expect to live like them. So, we want to survive as a nation and we want to be left alone as a nation. . . . We wish for the upcoming generation to survive in our future, and for them to carry on our identity, our language, and our culture. . . .
>
> We want to preserve our way of life, and we cannot do it with a pipeline. Right on our land. Any major developments that happen on our land. . . . We want to teach our children . . . how they can survive off the land if necessary . . . so that . . . when they do not have employment, with their education, they can go out somewhere where they can live prosperously also. That has not been the case in the past and there is a lot of unemployed people right now that are not entirely capable of handling themselves adequately in the bush.

One of the native people who took a different view of economic development in the Mackenzie region was trapper Alfred Lennie. Here is an extract from his testimony:

I have heard a lot of this meetings that have been going on and I have sat at meetings which I have heard with my two ears, and what I want to say is just a few words to make everybody understand what I want to say. . . .

I have grandchildren too. I have taken my kids out, which I have only got two and they are both married, and I have taken them out on the trapline and I have taught them how to trap, I have taught them how to hunt, and I taught them how to fish. But my kids won't come back and trap with me in the bush because they figured they had a little bit of education, and it is an easier life to go and get a job with the Government or somebody else. They make easier money.

. . . I have trapped all my life and right today I have seen grownup men . . . their parents are trappers . . . with education — do you see them going into the bush and trap? They are not trappers. They are looking for work. If there is a seismic line out here and an oil crew, that is where they go to look for a job.

I know for sure another, at least, say, ten years anyway, there will be no trappers because it is fading away right from my generation. . . . Why should our kids get educated and go and sit on the lake and set a fish net and freeze their fingers, when they have got education? Why should they do it?

So what I am thinking in my own right mind — I think that talking about this pipeline, I am not favouring the white man, I am not favouring anybody, I am favouring the future. If the pipelines goes through, the generation I am talking about, they're going to look for jobs off the pipeline, so that they can live because they cannot go into the bush and trap.

So why don't we come to a decision . . . rather than just fight against it and holler against it. . . . Let's settle the land claims settlement, get a royalty or something out of the land, and leave the land just the way it is. We are free to go where we want, we can shoot ducks closed season, we are happy just the way we are. Let's get something out of the land, and if they want to build the pipeline, let them build it so our kids and our grandchildren can work on that pipeline and they can earn themselves a living. Because they can't trap — I know that for sure.

Pipeline Development Policies

Both Mackenzie Valley pipeline applicants, Arctic Gas and Foothills groups, have developed extensive plans for offering as many economic benefits as possible to Northerners from construction and operation of the pipeline. Both, too, however, have made allowances in their plans to enable those Northerners who prefer to stick to the more traditional way of life in the North to do so.

An estimate based on end-of-1974 information suggested that there might be a pool of from 500 to 800 Northerners to draw from for the pipeline labour force. It was thought likely that all of these and more would be employed, if they wished, during the early stages of building the pipeline. During this time, as many as possible would be trained in skills they might use in later stages of construction, as heavy equipment operators, for instance. The construction phase should provide training opportunities for Northerners in skills that they might be able to use in the North on a continuing basis, after the pipeline is built — in such trades as electrical, plumbing and carpentry.

During the construction period of either pipeline proposal, the peak-year labour force demand was expected to be between 4,500 and 6,000 persons. Of these, about 40 per cent might be jobs that could be filled by non-experienced personnel capable of learning while they worked. Obviously there would not be enough Northerners to fill them all. To minimize the social and the economic impact of this huge temporary influx of southerners into the pipeline region to fill the jobs that the Northerners could not, outsiders would be housed in self-sufficient camps away from existing small communities.

Accommodation would also be provided for all permanent employees in the operation and management phases of the completed pipeline by the Trunk Line group, both for those in the Mackenzie region in connection with the Maple Leaf pipeline, and those in the Yukon for the Alaska Highway pipeline.

The purpose of these and similar policies was to meet the complaints of Northerners that temporary floods of southerners into their communities would cause social tensions, force up prices and create scarcities of services. Attempts to meet needs may lead to over-expansion, with consequent collapse of demand for them when the flood receded southwards again. These policies were also intended to reduce the impact of a permanent increase in the Northern population as a result of the pipeline.

175

The number of new jobs of a permanent nature expected to be created in the Mackenzie region by either pipeline project was the same — about 250. Since these would require skills many Northerners might not have, training-on-the job programs were planned which should, eventually, make it possible for all these jobs to be filled by Northerners. Possibly another 160 permanent jobs would be created by the establishment of plants in the Delta region to process the gas between wells and pipeline shipment. The potential producers, such as Imperial, Shell and Gulf, were training workers in the Nortran program in these skills. So were the pipeline companies. The number of lasting secondary jobs — those produced as a result of pipeline jobs — was estimated at anywhere from about 250 to 1,400 including possible work in further petroleum exploration inspired by the pipeline's existence.

The government guidelines also required that any pipeline contractor must tailor purchases of goods and services so as to allow bids from native organizations, settlement councils and Northern contractors wherever possible. Both applicant groups described to the NEB and the Berger Inquiry plans to do this, but in ways that would not falsely encourage existing Northern business to expand or new ones to establish capacities that might not be supported by demand after the pipeline is built. For this reason, Northern business entrepreneurs would be encouraged to expand according to long-term benefits from the operational, rather than the construction, phase.

The Foothills group put forward the same policies both for its Maple Leaf pipeline proposal up the Mackenzie Valley and its Alaska Highway pipeline proposal. To provide a vehicle for input for local businessmen, the Foothills group, through Foothills Pipe Lines, established a Pipeline Business Opportunities Board, composed of businessmen in the Mackenzie region. The board's objectives included determining sound business opportunities arising out of the proposed pipeline construction and operation, and promoting an awareness of these opportunities among the Northern communities, special interest groups and government and industry. The board was also assigned to facilitate communication both ways between Northern businessmen and the pipeline companies, including their construction contractors and subcontractors. A major purpose was to advise Foothills how to structure its project to maximize lasting benefits in the region.

176

It was estimated that production and transmission of gas from the Delta could produce enough taxation and royalty income to quickly wipe out the chronic deficit of federal government spending in the Northwest Territories. In the 1975-76 fiscal year, for instance, this deficit amounted to some $350 million — $189.5 million in federal contributions towards the Territorial government's expenditures of $216 million, and about $120 million in net direct federal spending in the Territory.

Gas for Northern Communities
One notable difference between the applications was the approach taken to provide natural gas for communities along the pipeline routes.

The Arctic Gas pipeline up the Mackenzie Valley would install valves and fittings at appropriate points to facilitate future construction of distribution facilities to serve Northern communities. Arctic Gas also expressed its willingness to co-operate with communities and industries that wished to use gas and to assist in planning and development of gas distribution facilities. However, it has advised the NEB that it does not intend to build, own or operate any gas distribution facilities in the Yukon or Northwest Territories (unless, of course, doing so was made a condition of its project approval — in which case the NEB and Government would also have to decide how these facilities should be paid for).

The Foothills group had always included in its planning a provision to connect Northern communities with gas from its main line in the Mackenzie Valley and the Yukon. The cost of building these lateral lines was included in the total cost estimates for the Maple Leaf project. The Foothills group also proposed that the gas be provided to these Northern communities at the same price as it would be delivered to connecting pipelines at the northern Alberta border.

Because of the distance most communities are from the proposed routes, and the relatively small demand for gas in them, few, if any, of the communities could afford the gas; the traditional utility approach is that consumers pay for the full cost of facilities required to produce and deliver the gas. The Foothills group proposed, instead, to add this service cost to the cost of delivering the much larger volumes to southern users.

8

CONCLUSIONS

The great Arctic gas pipeline drama is more than a story. It is a saga — a saga of powerful tycoons locked in a titanic struggle for more power; a saga of isolated native peoples made suspicious, confused and anxious about the prospects of so enormous a development crossing their lands, while at the same time enjoying an unprecedented opportunity for publicly proclaiming their nostalgia for a way of life which their own words reveal is already behind them. It is also the saga of an inner-directed judge and his inquiry staff, apparently anxious to leave a lasting imprint on the times.

This last chapter explores three areas which had an important bearing on the whole pipeline issue: the nature, influence and bias of the Berger Inquiry and its effect on the attitudes of native peoples of the North; the question of whether gas reserves made a pipeline economically feasible; and a last word on the history, status and nature of the two competing applications.

The Berger Inquiry
It could well be true, as Robert Blair and others had been saying for months, that no pipeline could be built up the Mackenzie Valley until the native land claims had been settled, and perhaps for sometime after that. If this is true, one of the main reasons is the Berger Inquiry and the unfortunate impact of its mingling of romanticism with reality. The Berger staff, evidently inspired by a messianic fervour, went at once beyond the mandate of the in-

quiry, which was to examine the impact of a pipeline in the Mackenzie regions on the people, birds, animals, fishes, ecosystems and environment.

There was an underlying assumption in the Berger Inquiry staff report that the white man could no more be trusted to change his ways with the native people today than in the past — though the existence of the inquiry itself was some evidence that the Canadian government's attitude towards native rights and wishes is not quite what it was in the past. Further evidence came from the government guidelines for Northern pipeliners and the extensive pains that the competing pipeline applicants have gone to in their plans for protecting the interests of the native people both in the construction and operation of their proposed projects.

There was recognition that beneficial changes are taking place in the native communities of the North in the Berger Inquiry staff report, but there was frequently a conflicting nostalgia for the old ways of the native peoples as well — a kind of yearning for some sort of Plato-like republic of the North, in which all change would cease, and the Mackenzie regions would become a vast museum peopled by natives turned back forever to their aboriginal lifestyles. Implied is an underlying doubt about the value of white civilization and the ability of the native peoples to maintain their own cultural and spiritual values as they find themselves drawn inevitably more and more into it, though the community hearings established that "native people sustain and hold fast to many values and activities they regard as traditional."

In the introduction to its November 1976 report the Berger Inquiry staff referred to "the competing and alternative realities that are raised by the pipeline project." But the inquiry, through its own processes, created some questionable "realities" itself. And the staff report created more. The staff report attempted to draw its own comprehensive blueprint for the future self-determination of the native peoples in the Yukon and Northwest Territories — and then urged the federal government to accept the recommendations whether or not a pipeline was built, and whether or not the land claims were ever settled.

"For," said the staff report, "these recommendations are directed towards problems that would be exacerbated by, but would not exclusively originate in the pipeline project, and which would be alleviated but might not be entirely solved by a land claims settlement."

What are these problems? They are real, but they are hardly new. They are the problems all people have had to solve when confronted with inescapable social change. And this is the underlying reality to be found in the pages of transcribed testimony by native people before the inquiry, if not necessarily always in the recommendations that resulted from the Inquiry. The native people in the Mackenzie regions, the transcripts show, are already well along an evolutionary journey moving them away from their aboriginal past.

In the testimony heard at Old Crow, there was evidence of improvements in the living conditions of the people which they welcome and appreciate: their school in which their children learn their native tongue; a nursing station and monthly visits from a doctor; an airstrip which meant that medicines could be flown in, people flown out to hospital, and more regular mail service. The old days when they were entirely dependent upon their beloved land were frequently filled with hardships and the threat of starvation. However, benefits of the white man's civilization have been accompanied by drawbacks — alcoholism the best-known of these.

Today, the testimony showed, the people of Old Crow are still able to hunt, trap and fish, but they also want to be able to work for wages — wages with which to buy the modern equipment that makes hunting, trapping and fishing easier and less rigorous than in the past. The residents of Old Crow were almost unanimously opposed to a pipeline passing anywhere near their ancient community, but this opposition influenced Arctic Gas in its decision to propose a route many miles north of Old Crow.

The Berger Inquiry staff did recognize the changing way of life that Northern natives are undergoing:

> Native peoples are for the most part no longer nomadic, and live for much of each year in fixed communities which were not established with a primary concern for their proximity to harvestable land resources. . . . At present, native people are not as completely dependent on the land and its resources, as in traditional times. . . . Moreover, earnings from wage-labor are regarded as important because they facilitate harvesting of local renewable resources through purchase of essential hunting gear, which now typically includes items such as outboard motors and skidoos. . . . The pipeline and related hydrocarbon develop-

There is that maketh himself rich, yet hath nothing: there is that maketh himself poor, yet hath great riches.

Proverbs 13:7

Friday   April 1996

19

ment could, given the right conditions, provide the native people with a further opportunity to use wage employment to maintain and strengthen their own economy.

In recognizing that the native people in the Mackenzie regions are no longer dependent upon their land for physical survival, the Berger staff report finds the benefits, limited and imperfect as they are, which they receive from their fellow Canadians, through the agencies of government, far more of a threat than a blessing. Because control over key functions like education, medicine and welfare has been "lifted" from the native people and "vested with large, impersonal government bureaucracies, the continuity and future of the traditional way of life is threatened," the report says.

In seeking ways "in which native society can, in its own terms, achieve the self-determination it wishes," the staff report came close to recommending new bureaucratic efforts to encourage the native peoples to return to their old lifestyle.

Some Northerners vigorously dispute the findings of the Berger Inquiry and views like those of Dr. Meyer Brownstone, president of Oxfam Canada, who said: "an economic development process which utilises wage labour is in fact counter-developmental." One Metis businessman, Joe Mercredi, who publishes a weekly newspaper in Fort Simpson, on the Mackenzie River, made pro-development submissions to the Berger Inquiry in Ottawa, Yellowknife and Fort Smith. In a Calgary newspaper interview at the end of March 1977, he complained bitterly about the way views like his were ignored in media coverage of the inquiry. (Calgary *Albertan* 31 March 1977) He was quoted as saying:

"Indian Brotherhood spokesmen [this includes Erasmus] are crying out that the exploitation of native peoples has got to stop. They want a land-claim settlement and a 20-year moratorium before any construction starts on the Mackenzie Valley pipeline. Yet there is a 78 per cent unemployment rate among natives in the North right now. So who's exploiting who?" The Metis Association and most of the native unemployed wanted work and that meant development.

He went on to say that the old native way of life was dead; that there was no reason why the native people, including the Metis, could not retain their culture, as do the Japanese-Canadians and Ukrainian-Canadians. "But you can't force an 1863 way of living on any people today — it simply doesn't exist any more."

In mid-April 1977, members of the Northwest Territories Council took a similar line against those trying to impose a falsely romanticized image on the North as it is today. One was Social Development Minister Peter Ernerk, himself an Inuit. Addressing graduation ceremonies for the corps of NWT interpreters in Yellowknife, he told them that the legislature supports settling the land claims and they had a vital job of explaining to their communities what their government was doing:

> The members of our legislature are trying their utmost to keep the people who live here united and cooperative, not split or separate according to social or ethnic backgrounds. The legislature is not in favour of setting up small states in the Northwest Territories, just as the federal government is not interested in seeing the province of Quebec separate from the rest of Canada . . . as long as the federal government continues to fund a multitude of political and special-interest groups in the Territories, the people of the NWT risk losing their opportunity to continue to develop responsible government. While our own legislature is asking the federal government to transfer more and more responsibility to the Territories, we are opposed continually by various organizations that claim to represent minority groups.

Unquestionably, the Berger Inquiry was a unique and valuable experiment in participatory — or advocatory? — democracy. The impact of the inquiry and the recommendations resulting from it for the most part should reinforce the new capitalist development ethic previously discussed. But was it as objective about the facts it accepted in the North as it might have been? One of these facts is that the North needs more development if Northerners, whether natives or not, are to enjoy a widened independence from paternalistic government assistance. Though this fact was certainly evident even in the inquiry staff report, the inquiry left an impression that any development in the North was likely to be bad for the native peoples.

The existence of the Berger Inquiry itself was witness to the fact that there certainly were strong new *intentions*, at least, of bringing a whole new approach to bear on future development in the North, starting with any pipeline which might be approved. If it is possible to plan resource development with a minimum of impact on the living habits of not only the people in a region but of birds, animals and fish, then this kind of planning has been done to an unprecidented extent for an Arctic gas pipeline. The past provided many sound reasons for scepticism, but the Berger Inquiry heard many sound *present* reasons for believing that we have entered a new era in the treatment of native peoples by the institutions of our predominantly white society's government.

But has the Berger Inquiry encouraged the native people to understand and believe this? Has it encouraged them to show the good faith on their side, which is just as essential as good faith on the government side, if this new era of equality and trust for the native people is to survive in sound health? Has the Berger Inquiry encouraged the native people to concentrate their attention on securing their present and future? Or has it encouraged them to negotiate their land claims and other rights and interests from a position clouded with nostalgia about a past which no one can reclaim now?

Gas Reserves

None of these comments about the Berger Inquiry are intended to be an argument in favour of any pipeline up the Mackenzie Valley at the present time. The native land claims and other worries about a pipeline aside, there is simply no sound economic reason to build a pipeline from the Mackenzie Delta to southern Canadian markets at this time. New discoveries and a new viability of known reserves in southern conventional areas as a result of price increases primarily have changed Canada's gas reserves picture again. We have enough gas from conventional sources — and evidently encouraging enough prospects of finding more — to meet Canada's needs, both for domestic demand and export contracts, well into the mid-1980s.

The five or six trillion cubic feet of gas reserves currently proven in the Mackenzie Delta are not enough to make either the Maple Leaf pipeline or the Arctic Gas piggyback proposal economically viable. Nor does the widely heard argument these days that without a pipeline from the Delta, exploration will cease, stand up to examination. All three of the major holders of reserves in the Delta — Shell, Gulf and Imperial — have advanced this argument. Shell announced plans to suspend drilling there until a gas pipeline was approved. Imperial Oil's annual report and statements by its president, J. A. Armstrong, said that Northern exploration would decline without a pipeline. Similar statements were made in the Gulf Oil Canada annual report.

It should be noted that all three of these companies were also members of the Arctic Gas consortium, and their parent companies were major holders of reserves in Alaska's Prudhoe Bay area. It should also be noted, as Judge Litt pointed out in his FPC report early in 1977, that no contracts had been signed by the producers with any southern distributors in the United States for sale of these Prudhoe Bay reserves.

The main leverage in this protracted pipeline struggle, aside from government powers, came from ownership of the gas to be shipped. Companies which owned gas reserves and also wanted to own a piece of any pipeline that might move those reserves to market were in a position to suggest they would only co-operate with the pipeline of their choice. They were in a position to suggest there might be delays — with convincing reasons — in construction of the processing plants required to treat the gas before it could be shipped, especially in a pipeline not of their choice. These are only two of the ways large multinational companies in the petroleum industry have of trying to influence government decisions concerning their interests.

The weakness of the argument that a decision not to build immediately a pipeline from the Delta would threaten future exploration there is this: there has never been a pipeline built anywhere until exploration efforts have found enough oil and/or gas to make the pipeline viable. If exploration in the Delta dwindles or ceases, there can be only three possible reasons. One is the exploration efforts to date have convinced the companies that there is no point in carrying on, an unlikely reason in this case. A second reason is that there are more accessible areas that promise better return on the companies' investment. This is a distinct possibility, because rising gas prices have made exploration in some of the more difficult areas of Alberta and British Columbia potentially attractive for the first time. A third reason is that threats of halting exploration may have been intended to persuade government that a Mackenzie Delta pipeline must go through.

There was also evidence at the end of March 1977 that backers of the Arctic Gas pipeline still entertained hopes that, by connecting Mackenzie Delta reserves to a pipeline carrying Alaska gas to the lower 48 states, the chances of being able to export these

Canadian reserves to the U.S. would be enhanced. The potential importance of these Canadian reserves to the U.S. was explained in late March 1977 to the U.S. House of Representatives subcommittee on Indian Affairs and Public Lands. This was the explanation given by Vern Horte, president of Canadian Arctic Gas Pipeline Limited:

> You must note that whereas Canada has reduced its oil exports — it has not cut off gas exports, which have been sold under long-term contracts. But as much as Canada should and does desire not to cut gas exports, the U.S. should desire it at least as much. Canadian gas is over 5 per cent of your gas supply, and much more than that of your interstate gas supply. It is of major importance in many of your northern states and California. In fact, you now get more Canadian gas than the volume of gas you will initially get from Prudhoe Bay. It would help you little if you hook up Prudhoe Bay, but lose all or part of the greater amount of Canadian gas because the Arctic Gas project is not approved and the Delta gas therefore cannot get to market by the early 1980s. If that occurs, Canada will have the choice of shorting its own markets or cutting exports. Neither of us should want that choice to be posed.

Other evidence of the determined interest of Arctic Gas backers in getting Canada's Mackenzie Delta gas into the U.S. was given before the National Energy Board. Gas sale and purchase contracts were filed before the board which showed that Shell, Gulf and Imperial Oil had undertaken to sell the greater part of their Canadian gas in the Beaufort Basin to U.S. transmission companies, and to Alberta and Southern Gas Company, a Calgary-based company controlled in California where it sells most of its gas. Only a minor amount of Delta gas had been disposed of to Trans-Canada PipeLines for Canadian consumption.

Last Word on the Applicants

It is not the intention of this book to advocate approval of either applicant group. But some facts are worth pointing out:

— Though it was established by the Alberta Goverment, Alberta Gas Trunk Line Limited is not an arm of the Alberta Government; it is an independent company with the majority of its directors chosen by its private shareholders. From the beginning, in fact, the provincial government had been nervous that Trunk

Line's involvement in this project might lead to a test of Alberta's constitutional right to regulate a pipeline system within the province which was devoted primarily to shipping gas across provincial and international boundaries — an area where the federal government clearly has constitutional primacy. And whether Trunk Line or Arctic Gas built the pipeline across Alberta, the provincial economy would feel almost the same beneficial impact to its growth.

— Though the Toronto-based executives of Arctic Gas denied it, there was no doubt that Arctic Gas has been, is and would continue to be, if approved, dominated by American companies, primarily Exxon, with Gulf and Shell close behind. The voting procedure of the Arctic Gas group guarantees this, for its board of directors is divided into three groups, each with effective veto power over any decision, to ostensibly protect the interests of Canadian companies in the consortium. However, this procedure has also given the gas producers (primarily Exxon, Gulf and Shell) on the board the same veto power — and their interests may be expected to be more cohesive than the interests of others on the board. With this veto power, the consortium could be forced to operate with the gas producers' interests foremost.

— On the other hand, there was equally no doubt that the financial structure proposed for both the Alaska Highway and Maple Leaf pipelines would ensure Canadian equity ownership and management control of the Canadian sections of both these pipelines unless they could not be financed at all, which was an unlikely possibility. Nor was there much doubt that these projects would be easier to finance, especially separately, with several years separating their construction, than the massive, one-stage effort of Arctic Gas. This would hold even truer if there was no economic justification for building any pipeline out of the Delta.

— If Arctic Gas should win this project, much of the credit should go to its public affairs director, former Calgarian A. Earle Gray, for his public relations program outclassed that of the Foothills group on every front. Talks with members of Parliament, the Parliamentary Press Gallery and representatives of other influential groups, including some in Trunk Line's hometown of Calgary, left no doubt about the success of the Arctic Gas public relations efforts. Nearly everyone I spoke to who knew anything at all about the Arctic gas pipeline stakes seemed under the impression that only Arctic Gas was a serious applicant.

186

There seemed little awareness that Trunk Line initiated the plan for training Northerners to work on the pipeline, by itself in 1970 — a plan Arctic Gas supported to the end and usually claimed as its own. Or that Trunk Line initially established the Environmental Protection Board with a unique independence which was swiftly removed when it came under the control of Arctic Gas. There seemed little awareness that one project would be Canadian-owned and controlled, whereas the other would move the balance of control over Canadian pipelines — now predominantly Canadian-held — into the U.S. Least of all did there seem to be much awareness of the size, capacity and achievement of the two major participants in the Alaska Highway and Maple Leaf proposals, Westcoast Transmission and Trunk Line. This sometimes led to an expression of doubt about their capacity to build the projects which they proposed.

The evidence clearly demonstrates that any such doubts are the result of ignorance and bad communication; they have no basis in fact.

Westcoast began building pipelines in British Columbia and Trunk Line in Alberta in 1956. Between them they operate 7,750 miles of gas pipelines, most of them 42 inches in diameter. During the last five years, they financed $540 million worth of new pipelines — about $170 million more than the entire cost of TransCanada PipeLine. Much of this mileage was built, often during cold weather, through Northern terrain, and some in permafrost zones. From the beginning of their pipeline building to the end of 1976, Westcoast and Trunk Line between them had built $1.4 billion worth of gas pipelines altogether.

The western Canadian sedimentary basis is estimated to hold well over 100 trillion cubic feet of gas reserves. This makes it one of the very largest in North America. Trunk Line and Westcoast, as exclusive gatherers and transporters of gas from this basin, distribute most of the gas produced in Canada, including all of the one trillion cubic feet currently being exported to the U.S. Among North American pipelines, Trunk Line ranks second only to the American Tenneco pipeline in the amount of gas that moves through its system, which in 1977 should be about two trillion cubic feet, and its capacity is increasing.

Because they are constantly expanding their pipeline systems, Trunk Line and Westcoast each has its own design engineering and construction management, instead of relying on outside consultants. Trunk Line, in fact, maintains the largest gas or oil pipeline design and engineering management organization in Canada. Taken with their jointly sponsored subsidiary, Foothills Pipe Lines Limited, Trunk Line and Westcoast together have certainly the largest and most experienced pipeline engineering unit in Canada, and possibly in the world.

This helps to explain why, though it seemed little appreciated outside the environs of the National Energy Board, the two-pipeline proposal of the Foothills group was superior in several ways to the Arctic Gas group's proposal for a single pipeline. The record showed that the Foothills group pipelines were of a simpler, more tested engineering design (especially where frost-heave problems were concerned), would be easier to finance without government backing, would cause less environmental disruption by avoiding a *crossing* of the North Slope of Alaska and the Yukon and the Mackenzie Delta, would be faster to build by using existing corridors, would be less likely to have damaging breaks at a pressure of 1,250 or 1,260 pounds per square inch than its opponent's at 1,680, and would run less risk of going far over cost estimates. The greater attention paid to socio-economic issues by the Foothills group from the beginning promised a better performance in this area, too, from the Calgary-based group. Furthermore, if they went ahead at all, the Canadian sections of the Foothills group's pipelines would be financed, built, owned, operated and controlled by Canadians, not an international consortium dominated from outside Canada.

Finally, it is fascinating to note — despite the unprecendented spending and activity on pre-project planning — the crucial role that chance played in this long-running drama.

A pipeline from Prudhoe Bay along the Alyeska Corridor and Alaska Highway was the idea of none of the companies involved. It was the brainchild of a professor of economics at the University of Alaska, who also acted as a consultant to the U.S. Senate Committee on Energy and Natural Resources, Dr. Arlen Tussing, who was not connected with any of the competing companies. He buttonholed Blair during a Washington visit in February 1976 to plead with him to give some serious thought to the idea. Blair at first bridled at the idea. It would have to be put forward by an American company since it would depend upon U.S. approval to succeed and furthermore, Blair initially saw Tussing's idea as a possible threat to the Maple Leaf project.

Blair did, however, agree to consider it, and on his return to Calgary, he mentioned it to Gibson, who immediately became enthusiastic about it. Gibson, in turn, saw that the idea was taken up with Northwest Pipeline in Salt Lake City, whose executives also became immediately interested. Finally, pressure from Westcoast and Northwest persuaded Blair to bring Trunk Line's support behind this proposal, as well as the Maple Leaf project.

Tussing gave his reasons for advocating the Alyeska corridor-Alaska Highway route during a March 1977 appearance in Washington before the subcommittee on Indian affairs and public lands of the U.S. House of Representatives' committee on the Interior. They may be summarized as follows:

All three proposals — Arctic Gas, Alaska Highway and El Paso — were likely to experience cost overruns, but Arctic Gas had the greatest potential for these because its route was relatively unknown and it relied upon unproven technology.

Arctic Gas might end up costing $20 billion instead of the estimated $10 to $12 billion with a consequent higher delivery cost to southern consumers.

The Alaska Highway project had the least potential for cost overruns because its route was well known and did not rely on untested techniques.

In terms of potential for cost overruns, El Paso ranked between the others, but it was not an acceptable alternative because it involved the costly process of liquefying the gas, and would then dump all of it in California, whereas the other projects would spread the gas across the continent.

There was unlikely to be any Mackenzie Valley pipeline in the near future for two reasons: vast amounts of gas reserves were available in Alberta and British Columbia, removing the urgency for Canada to connect the Mackenzie Delta reserves, and the Berger Inquiry was expected to recommend against any Mackenzie Valley pipeline in the foreseeable future, creating a political objection which the Canadian government was unlikely to override.

As both the American and Canadian supporters of the Alaska Highway project still believed, a 42-inch-diameter pipeline was the largest that proven gas reserves at Prudhoe Bay justified on technical and financial grounds; if a larger-diameter line were approved, it would be over-sized for the available gas supplies and would require government financial support to build.

189

ALASKA HIGHWAY VARIATION
WITH DEMPSTER HIGHWAY

TERRITORIES

TRANSCANADA PIPELINES

innipeg

Emerson

Quebec City

GREAT LAKES

Montreal

Ottawa

MIDWESTERN

Toronto

The idea of using existing pipeline systems in British Columbia and Alberta and perhaps the TransCanada system and its connection at Emerson, Manitoba, to the existing Great Lakes system in the midwestern U.S. was an attractive alternative to other proposals. Further, a decision on exactly what additional capacity to build in Canada and the lower U.S. could be delayed until more was known about how much Alaskan gas would be deliverable and when.

No matter what facilities were built — whether a new express line or a combination of new line and looping of existing lines — and no matter what route was finally chosen, the Foothills group's principle of segmenting responsibility for the project among several companies should be followed, as opposed to placing total responsibility with one project company, as proposed by Arctic Gas. In any event, existing operating companies in B.C. and Alberta — that is Westcoast Transmission and Trunk Line — should have responsibility for the construction and operation of all facilities in their areas. This approach would lead to sound management of the project and limit the potential for cost overruns.

President Jimmy Carter was expected to recommend approval by Congress of a hybrid system, not exactly like any of the projects proposed.

In Ottawa at mid-April, I found a wide awareness among influential people of the ideas of Tussing. This helped me to recognize the obvious solution — a solution in which another key element of chance figured.

At the request of the NEB, the competing applicant groups produced in late March 1977 several other possible methods of connecting Mackenzie Delta gas to the south. One of these, from Foothills, was for a variation of the Alaska Highway proposal, which would reroute that proposed pipeline between Delta Junction in Alaska and Whitehorse in the Yukon. Instead of following the Alaska Highway entirely, this alternative would either proceed due east across country from Delta Junction or follow the Taylor Highway from Tetlin Junction northeasterly to the Yukon border, then the Boundary Road east to Dawson, and from there along the Klondike Highway south to Whitehorse. The Delta gas could then be connected to this line through a 30-inch-diameter pipeline along the Dempster Highway to its junction with the Klondike Highway.

This alternate route would add about 65 miles to the Alaska Highway project if it went cross-country from Delta Junction, or

120 miles if it followed the Taylor Highway from Tetlin Junction. But a Dempster Highway pipeline from the Delta to the junction with the Klondike Highway would be 276 miles shorter than if it had to be built to connect with the Alaska Highway pipeline at Whitehorse — a distance of 460 miles compared to 736 miles. Either way, of course, a Dempster Highway route would be shorter than the 817 miles of Maple Leaf or roughly the same length of Arctic Gas pipeline that would have to be built up the Mackenzie Valley to connect Delta gas via that route with existing pipeline systems or new line at the northern borders of Alberta and British Columbia. A rough estimate was that the shorter Dempster Highway route would cost about $2 billion, compared to $4.6 billion for the Maple Leaf line, but the Dawson alteration in the Alaska Highway project would add to the $7.3 billion estimated cost of that proposal — by how much was not included in this study.

This alternate of a Dawson variation in the Alaska Highway route, with a possible Delta connection via the Dempster Highway, did not turn up entirely by chance, but it was not produced by the main planning process of either applicant group. Out of all the information to be weighed in connection with the formal proposals, this relatively last-minute development seemed by April 1977 to be the most promising solution to the issues left to the Canadian and U.S. governments to settle. The logical solution began to seem obvious.

The lower 48 states of the U.S. should be connected as quickly as possible with Alaskan gas from Prudhoe Bay. There is no immediate justification for any pipeline south from the Mackenzie Delta. A pipeline from Prudhoe Bay south along the Alyeska Corridor and the Alaska Highway, with a jog up to Dawson on the way, would probably bring Alaskan gas to markets in the U.S. more quickly and less expensively and with less environmental effect than any other project.

This would then free Canada from any immediate need to build a pipeline from the Mackenzie Delta, which is not needed either by southern consumers or justified economically by known reserves, and seems currently unacceptable politically. But this variation of the Alaska Highway project would ensure that if (and when) Delta reserves are required, they could be connected to southern Canada by the shortest and least expensive route, along an existing transportation corridor which would minimize its impact on the environment.

No pipeline should be built up the Mackenzie Valley at the

present time — not because of the native land claims, which the James Bay settlement showed *can* be fairly negotiated while development is going on, but because there are not enough proven reserves in the Delta to warrant a pipeline, especially when southern reserves are going begging for markets.

A decision along the lines proposed here was made easier for Canada by the recommendations of the U.S. Federal Power Commission to President Carter on May 2. The four members of the FPC in effect advised the President that either the Arctic Gas or the Alaska Highway project was acceptable to the U.S., but the weight of the FPC recommendations seemed slightly in favour of the Alaska Highway route.

This route was favoured by the FPC chairman, Richard Dunham, and the vice-chairman, James Watt. Commissioners John Hollman and Don Smith preferred the Arctic Gas proposal. In the words of the FPC letter to Carter: ". . . conditioned upon timely affirmative decisions by the Government of Canada to make the (Arctic Gas) route available and, after development, to allow simultaneous transportation of Canadian natural gas reserves from the Mackenzie Delta." The two commissioners added: "In the absence of a Canadian determination that development and transportation of Mackenzie reserves should be permitted, the Alcan project should be approved, subject to the Government of Canada's making the route available on acceptable terms and conditions."

All four FPC members recommended either overland route over El Paso's proposal to move Alaska gas south by pipeline and ship. They also estimated that both the Alaska Highway and Arctic Gas projects would cost more than El Paso, using their own FPC estimates and not the figures provided by the applicants. They found that Arctic Gas had the greatest risk of major cost overruns, primarily because of its winter construction schedule, but if Delta gas were also developed and the Arctic Gas pipeline shared by Canadian and Alaskan gas, Arctic Gas' cost of service to Americans would be slightly below those of the Alaska Highway system. They advised the President that if Canada decides not to develop its Delta reserves at this time, the overall balance of cost advantages shifts to the Alaska Highway project.

As Canadian Energy Minister Alastair Gillespie commented in Ottawa, the FPC recommendations left all the options open for the Canadian Government.

EPILOGUE

BERGER'S IMPOSSIBLE DREAM

To any political realist, the report by Mr. Justice Thomas Berger
on his Mackenzie Valley Pipeline Inquiry came as no surprise, but
as a profound disappointment. It was as romantically utopian as
his conduct of the inquiry. By almost totally rejecting political
realism, an approach perhaps not unexpected from a man with a
socialist background, he threw away a unique opportunity to
recommend attainable improvements in the Canadian democratic
system of government, especially in the protection and fostering of
minority rights. Instead of contributing to the *evolution* of Canadian democracy, Berger advocated a *revolutionary* change in the
Canadian constitution to give the native peoples of the North "a
special status," one which most other Canadians are likely to
reject.

The proposals by the pipeline companies for protecting the
interests of Northerners if a pipeline were built up the Mackenzie
Valley, were in some ways more realistic and practical (if not so
grandiose) than Berger's, and therefore more likely to have been of
actual benefit. Though Berger's report both over-estimates and
under-estimates the impact of a Mackenzie Valley pipeline on the
native economy of the North, the economic impact of the pipeline
would probably, though relatively modest in the long-run, be more
beneficial for all Northerners than Berger's recommended 10-year
moratorium on industrial development.

Berger's report tabled in the House of Commons 9 May 1977

went far beyond the mandate of the inquiry. The federal cabinet order of 21 March 1974 instructed him to "inquire into and report upon the terms and conditions that should be imposed" on any pipeline up the Mackenzie Valley, "having regard to the regional social, environmental and economic impact." Berger's recommendations, if fully implemented by government, would be tantamount to a re-ordering of Canadian Confederation — resulting perhaps in near anarchy — and have little to do with pipelines.

Berger reveals that he wants to influence future relations between whites and native peoples, not only in the Mackenzie regions, but in all Canada. He quotes approvingly Andre Siegfried's reference to the North as "a window which opens out on to the infinite" and says: "It may be that, through this window, we shall discover something of the shape that our future relations with the native people of our country must assume." He claims even more for his report with "we have the opportunity to make a new departure, to open a new chapter in the history of the indigenous peoples of the Americas."

Berger, like his staff, was not satisfied to assess the impact of a pipeline on the northern people, their economy and environment, and to recommend how it might be built to minimize harmful effects and gain the most benefit. He seems unable to resist the temptation to assume the role of saviour of a way of life of northern natives that is opposed to the capitalist industrial system — but a way of life his own hearings found had already slipped back into history.

"This is not retreat into the past," Berger claims of his report and its recommendations. In a sense this is true: the report is a full-scale advance into the past. His report advocates turning back the North's evolutionary clock almost "to the infinite."

Example:

He states that "the evolution of political institutions in the Northwest Territories since 1905 has followed the pattern of the provinces." At another point he notes that "the concept of native self-determination [which Berger unconditionally supports] is antithetical to the vision of the future held by many white people in the Northwest Territories, who believe that, in due course, the Territories should become a province like the other provinces." Berger's implied suggestion is that the Territories not become a province like the others, but should be turned over to the native peoples "whether by establishment of native institutions on a geographical basis or by the transfer of certain functions of the Government of Canada and the Government of the Northwest Territories to native institutions.'' With this recommendation, Berger would turn back the North at least to 1905.

Example:

In recommending that the Arctic Gas pipeline not be built across the northern Yukon, along either the proposed coastal route or the inland route passing near Old Crow, Berger also recommended that "a new kind of park" be established in that area. The park would extend across the entire Yukon Territory from the Porcupine River northward to the Arctic coast, including Herschel Island and all other islands adjoining the coast. Its northern boundary would be three miles offshore. Berger rightly describes this as a "unique area of wilderness" and quotes Dr. George Calef's description of it (from *The Urgent Need for a Canadian Arctic Wildlife Range*:

> . . . a land richer in wildlife, in variety of landscape and vegetation, and in archaeological value than any other in the Canadian Arctic. Here high mountains, spruce forests, tundra, wide 'flats' of lakes and ponds, majestic valleys . . . and the arctic seacoast come together to form the living fabric of the arctic wilderness. Altogether there are nine million acres of spectacular land in its natural state, inhabited by thriving populations of northern plants and animals including some species which are in serious danger elsewhere.

Obviously, this proposed "wilderness park" is an attractive proposition except possibly to Arctic Gas and other industrial interests. In Berger's words:

> It would afford absolute protection to wilderness and the environment by excluding all industrial activity within it. Of course there would have to be guarantees permitting the native people to continue to live and to carry on their traditional activities within the park without interference. . . . The size and boundaries of the proposed park would protect important habitats of migrating birds, the Porcupine caribou herd, and various other mammals; they would also protect the most important hunting and trapping areas of the Old Crow people and the unique wilderness area of the northern Yukon. The park would include the Yukon coastal plain and the Old Crow flats. The Canadian sector of the Porcupine caribou herd's spring and summer range

and the critically important calving range of the herd would lie within it.

It would indeed be a new kind of park, "new" in that not only would it protect the birds, animals and fish but the native peoples within it would be frozen into the infinite, practising their "traditional activities." Whether such a park would turn back, or even freeze, the evolution of native society is doubtful for in the history of man, there has been no "absolute protection" of anything or anyone. So how can a native way of life that began disappearing last century be restored and forever protected?

Example:

Berger rightly finds fault with the kind of education that white society has provided for northern natives in the past, but concedes: "It is not to be denied that the new education brought advantages. Without it, native people would have been even less able to understand and cope with the changes taking place in the North and with the new institutional and administrative forms that were being imposed on them." By implication he rejects the statement by the Northwest Territories department of education that it is not pursuing today a program of cultural assimilation, and discounts the evidence his inquiry heard that native interests are being given a new importance in the northern education system.

The report says: "The native people are not in doubt on this issue. They say that, as long as the system is run by white people, it will reflect white views of what the northern curriculum ought to be. The native people argue that since its inception, the purpose of the government's education program in the North has been to assimilate them." Berger obviously believes this although it has not been true, at least since the native peoples' rejection of the federal white paper on native policy in 1969. Although his own inquiry is eloquent evidence of the government's willingness today to listen to and respond to the wishes of the native peoples, Berger takes the position that no good for native peoples can come out of the existing system, so instead of recommending improvements in it, he advocates its total replacement.

Berger notes that current education policy in the North "provides for instruction to native children in their mother tongue during the first three years of school," but acknowledges that this has not yet come about because there are not enough native teachers available to teach the native languages.

Somehow he concludes that by ''the transfer from the territorial government to the native people of all authority over the education of native children,'' this situation will be improved, although he compliments the Territories department of education which ''has sincerely tried to establish an education system that would reflect Dene and Inuit desires. Its administrators, supervisors and teachers are dedicated educators.'' But, ''with the best will in the world and with ample funds, the department has not succeeded in fulfilling the Dene and Inuit desires as yet'' and, ''there are no grounds for believing that it will ever succeed.''

Berger believes that ''one people cannot run another people's schools.'' The extent of transfer of control from the Territories government to native control is something he says should be resolved by negotiation. ''But it must be clearly understood that the transfer of control is not merely a decentralization of power under the general supervision of the Territorial government — that would only perpetrate the existing state of affairs. The transfer of control must be real, and it must occur at all levels.''

There is no sound reason for opposing the control by native peoples over their education curriculum and for including in it such subjects as native history, skills, lore and native rights, along with native languages, as Berger proposes. But his fascination with building political dams to divert social evolution from forward to backward is again evident in his suggestion that eventually white children as well as native children should be required to attend native schools in native communities. He cannot seem to bring himself to believe that progress can be made through evolutionary change. His political faith seems ever to depend on revolutionary change, and usually in the direction of the past.

Berger is probably right when he says: ''Because the native people think it is important for their children to learn English, as well as to preserve their own language, and to learn about white culture as well as to preserve their own, it is likely that white children who have spent a few years in such a school system would not suffer any disadvantage from it, and that in many ways they would benefit from the experience.'' But the utopian's temptation to force people to do what is best for them, whether they want it or not, shines through the next sentence: ''It would also mean that only white families who have a genuine interest in the North and its people would choose to live in the native villages.''

Berger is under no illusion that his report constitutes an unprecendented attempt by an inquiry, established by the existing order of liberal capitalist democracy, to change that order. The native peoples whose view he supports are attempting "to alter the political, economic and social order of the Northwest Territories," and he says, whites "are right to regard this as an attempt to change the existing order."

"But they should not resent it, because a growing native consciousness is a fact of life in the North. It was bound to come. It is not going to go away, even if we impose political institutions in which it has no place." And of course Berger had done his skillful best with his inquiry and report to ensure that the institutions imposed are those he favours.

There are frequent examples of Berger's failure to recognize the change in political approach to development in the North today. There is in this statement an assumption that the future must be the prisoner of past experience: "Both the white and the native people in the North realize that the government's decision on the pipeline and on the way in which native claims are settled, will determine whether the political evolution of the North will follow the pattern of the history of the West or whether it will find a place for native ideas of self-determination." Again, the very existence of Berger's own inquiry is evidence enough that the political evolution of the North is already moving in quite a different pattern from that of the West.

Nor does Berger ever really explain why this statement should be taken as seriously as he makes it: "The settlement of native claims must be the point of departure for any political reorganization in the Northwest Territories. That is why the decision on the pipeline is really a decision about the political future of the Northwest Territories. . . . The native people throughout the Mackenzie Valley and the Western Arctic sense that the decision on the pipeline is the turning point in their history. For them the time of decision has arrived."

If the pipeline decision marks a watershed in the history of northern natives, it will be because Berger set out to make it so, not because it is inherently so. Berger himself is contradictory on the extent of the pipeline's potential impact on the economy of the North. At one point he says: "The construction of the pipeline now will entail a commitment by the Government of Canada and the Government of the Northwest Territories to a program of large-scale frontier development, which, once begun, cannot be diverted from its course. Once construction begins, the concentration on the non-renewable resource sector and the movement away from the renewable resource sector will become inexorable. The goal of strengthening the native economy will be frustrated." Elsewhere in the report, he argues that the pipeline will have a temporary economic impact during its construction period and then this impact will subside as the impact of previous large projects in the North has done. And at another point, he says the pipeline "would bring only limited economic benefits."

There is much useful information about the North and the native traditions in Berger's unique report, and some useful suggestions. He is probably right when he forecasts that the pipeline construction would bring many new social pressures and tensions and problems to the North, though considering all the measures planned to minimize them, there must be some doubt that building a pipeline "would do enormous damage to the social fabric of the North," as Berger claims.

The fatal flaw in Berger's report is that he cannot believe that there is any way for the native economy and the industrial economy to develop in harmony in the North, though his inquiry heard evidence that this is already happening, if not fast enough for anyone's satisfaction. Berger says he does not want to suggest that "native people will not want to participate in the opportunities for employment that industrial development will create. Some native people already work alongside workers from the South. Many native people have taken advantage of opportunities for wage employment — particularly in the Delta — on a seasonal basis to obtain the cash they need to equip or re-equip themselves for traditional pursuits." At another point he reports an argument his inquiry heard: "The industrialization of the North has already begun, and it will continue and will force further changes upon the native people. The power of technology to effect such changes cannot be diminished, nor can its impact be arrested." But many of his recommendations are intended at least to hold back this power, if not stop it altogether, in the North.

Berger says of the native people themselves: "They acknowledge the benefits we have brought to them. They say that they are, in some respects, more comfortable now than they were in the old days. The industrial system has provided many things that they value, such as rifles, radios, outboard motors and snowmobiles." But Berger keeps coming back to his worry about change in the

North. And he identifies the chief perpetrator of it: "the great agency of change in the North is the presence of industrial Man."

And so Berger recommends as the major protection against industrial change a 10-year moratorium, along with a special status for the northern natives. He advocates a position of privilege for the native peoples in the North beyond anything ever granted to any element of Canadian society. If the right to self-determination which Berger advocates for Northern natives were applied across the nation it would lead to political chaos and the breakup of Canada in anarchistic confusion.

He writes:

> I do not say that industrial development should not take place. . . . it is taking place. But unless we decide that, as a matter of priority, a firmly strengthened renewable resource sector must be established in the Mackenzie Valley and Western Arctic, we shall not see a diversified economy in the North. Non-renewable resources need not necessarily be the sole basis of the northern economy in the future. We should not place absolute faith in any model of development requiring large-scale technology. . . . The renewable resource sector must have priority over the economic development of the North.

Nowhere does he give any reason for this conclusion except that some of the native peoples demand it. Nor does he anywhere prove that the native economy and the industrial economy cannot continue to develop together in the North, with the latter perhaps even supporting the other for more rapid development in the future. What seems to prevent Berger from believing that this could happen, and recommending how it might happen more effectively, is his wariness of the capitalist industrial economy. His report advocates a socialist-style economy based on the native tradition of cooperation, more than it supports the liberal capitalist democracy based on competition that we have in Canada today.

Instead of making useful recommendations for sensible and realizable improvements in the circumstances of northern natives, Berger advocates a social and political revolution in the North that cannot win complete acceptance in the rest of Canada — not even in the North. By fostering unrealistic expectations among native peoples, Berger may well have undermined their future and prepared the way for new misunderstandings and disputes between native and white societies in Canada, instead of trying to smooth their separate but inseparable futures.

How can there be anything but disappointment for those who share Berger's romantic tendencies in political evaluations, when it becomes evident that the evolutionary clock *cannot* be turned back, but can only be adjusted toward the future?

If history teaches any lesson, it is that human progress is usually best made by reforming or renovating or rebuilding existing structures; the radical approach that everything must be first torn down and then entirely new structures erected usually serves only to delay real progress, and often to create new problems as bad as the old, or worse. Yet this is what Berger seems to advocate when he claims the native people of the North want a new Confederation, a fundamental reordering of relations between themselves and the rest of Canada. If the northern natives have this right, why not natives in all of Canada? Why not all Canadians?

The most telling comment on the Berger report may well have come from Rick Hardy of the Northwest Territories Metis Association the day the report was make public, when he said that delay in industrial development that Berger recommends, would doom the Mackenzie Valley to "a welfare economy."

The native peoples deserve fair treatment on their land claims and a wider say in their education system, and many other improvements in the long-neglected role they have had to play in Canadian history, but if they take seriously every one of Berger's recommendations, there might well be the civil disturbance in the North, that Berger's report suggests is possible.

For what Berger seems most likely to have succeeded in doing, both in his conduct of his inquiry and in his report, is to have built for the native peoples of the North an impossible dream.

CHRONOLOGY

1967 — TransCanada PipeLines Limited of Toronto, Michigan Wisconsin Pipe Line Company of Detroit, and Natural Gas Pipeline Company of America, Chicago, initiate a feasibility study of a natural gas pipeline from the Liard Basin in the southwestern region of the Northwest Territories.

1968 — Oil and gas are discovered by Atlantic Richfield Company of Los Angeles on the North Slope of Alaska, overlooking Prudhoe Bay in the Arctic Ocean.

1969 — Oil and gas are discovered by Panarctic Oils Limited of Calgary in Canada's Arctic islands off the Mackenzie Delta.

— Westcoast Transmission Company Limited of Vancouver and Bechtel Corporation of San Francisco form Mountain Pacific Pipeline Limited to consider building an Arctic gas pipeline.

1970 — The TransCanada group expands its study to examine the feasibility of a pipeline south from Prudhoe Bay and the Mackenzie Delta, and adds to its membership: Atlantic Richfield, Standard Oil Company (Sohio) of Cleveland, and Humble Oil and Refining Company of New York and Houston.

— Alberta Gas Trunk Line Limited of Calgary attempts unsuccessfully to join TransCanada group, then begins its own study of a pipeline from Prudhoe Bay and the Mackenzie Delta. It is joined by Columbia Gas System Incorporated of Wilmington, Northern Natural Gas Company of Omaha, Texas Eastern Transmission Corporation of Houston, Canadian National Railways, and Pacific Lighting Gas Development Company of Los Angeles.

1972 — TransCanada and Trunk Line groups merge; total membership eventually reaches 28:

      Alberta Gas Trunk Line Limited
      Alberta Natural Gas Company Limited
      Atlantic Richfield Company
      Canada Development Corporation
      Canadian National Railways
      Canadian Pacific Investments Limited
      Canadian Superior Oil Limited
      Canadian Utilities
      Colorado Interstate Corporation
      Columbia Gas Transmission Corporation
      Consumers Gas Company
      Exxon (Humble Oil and Refining Company Limited)
      Gulf Oil Canada Limited
      Imperial Oil Limited
      Michigan Wisconsin Pipe Line Company
      Natural Gas Pipeline Company of America
      Northern and Central Gas Corporation Limited
      Northern Natural Gas Company
      Numac Oil and Gas
      Pacific Lighting Gas Development Company
      Panhandle Eastern Pipe Line Company
      Pembina Pipe Line Limited
      Shell Canada Limited
      Standard Oil Company (Sohio)
      Texas Eastern Transmission Corporation
      TransCanada PipeLines Limited
      Trans Continental Gas Pipeline Corporation
      Union Gas Limited

1974 — Alberta Gas Trunk Line withdraws from the Trans-Canada group and joins with Westcoast Transmission to establish jointly-owned Foothills Pipe Lines Limited of Calgary, in support of the Maple Leaf pipeline south to

Canadian markets from Canadian gas wells in the Mackenzie Delta.

1976 — Northwest Pipeline Corporation of Salt Lake City and the Foothills group propose a pipeline to move Prudhoe Bay gas to the lower 48 United States via the Alyeska corridor and Alaska Highway. The Foothills group would build Canadian sections and a Northwest subsidiary, Alcan Pipeline Company, the Alaskan section.

1977 — Arctic Gas group (Canadian Arctic Gas Pipeline Limited) membership stands at 15:

> Alberta Natural Gas Company Limited
> Columbia Gas Transmission Corporation
> Consumers' Gas Company
> Gulf Oil Canada Limited
> Imperial Oil Limited
> Michigan Wisconsin Pipe Line Company
> Natural Gas Pipeline Company of America
> Northern and Central Gas Corporation Limited
> Northern Natural Gas Company
> Pacific Lighting Gas Development Company
> Panhandle Eastern Pipe Line Company
> Shell Canada Limited
> Texas Eastern Transmission Corporation
> TransCanada PipeLines Limited
> Union Gas Limited

— Foothills group:

> Alberta Gas Trunk Line Limited
> Alcan Pipeline Company
> Foothills Pipe Lines Limited
> Foothills Pipe Lines (Yukon) Limited
> Northwest Pipeline Corporation
> Westcoast Transmission Company Limited

BIBLIOGRAPHY

Alberta Gas Trunk Line files.

Arctic Gas Pipeline Company Limited weekly digest.

An Energy Strategy for Canada, Queen's Printer, Ottawa, 1976.

"The Environment Protection Board Concept — Gas Arctic Systems," D. W. Craik, and Dr. George Calef, Paper No. 7258, Petroleum Society of Canadian Institute of Metallurgy.

Northern Frontier, Northern Homeland: the Report of the Mackenzie Valley Inquiry Vol. 1 by Mr. Justice Thomas R. Berger.

"Pipelining and People in the Arctic," Lee G. Hurd, Northwest Project Study Group. Paper No. SPE 3284, Society of Petroleum Engineers of AIME delivered in Chicago in April 1971.

Report of Berger Inquiry staff's "Commission Counsel Submissions," Toronto, October 1976.

Studies, briefs and transcripts of testimony submitted before the Federal Power Commission of the United States.

Studies, briefs and transcripts of testimony submitted before the National Energy Board of Canada.

Transcripts of testimony before the Mackenzie Valley Pipeline (Berger) Inquiry.

INDEX